Of Morsels and Marvels

THE AFRICA LIST

MARYSE CONDÉ

Of Morsels and Marvels

TRANSLATED BY RICHARD PHILCOX

Seagull
BOOKS

LONDON NEW YORK CALCUTTA

The work is published with the support of the
Publication Assistance Programmes of the Institut français

Seagull Books, 2020

Originally published in French as *Mets et merveilles*
© Éditions Jean-Claude Lattès, 2015

First published in English translation by Seagull Books, 2020
English translation © Richard Philcox, 2020

ISBN   978 0 8574 2 693 2

British Library Cataloguing-in-Publication Data
A catalogue record for this book is available from the British Library

Typeset by Seagull Books, Calcutta, India
Printed and bound by WordsWorth India, New Delhi, India

CONTENTS

As the year 2011 drew to a close while I was still teaching in New York, Mary-Ann Caws asked me for four recipes—two cocktails without alcohol and two desserts. Mary-Ann Caws, professor of French literature and modern art at the City University's Graduate Center, is one of the most extraordinary women I have met. She is a brilliant speaker and can talk engagingly on André Breton, Pablo Picasso, Salvador Dali, Robert Desnos and René Char. She uses the same talent to write about the novels of Virginia Woolf, literary manifestos and Provençal cuisine. This time she was compiling a book of painters' and writers' recipes for an English publisher under the title *Modern Art Cookbook*. My first reaction was: Why me? She merely replied: 'Because your cooking is one of the best I have ever tasted.' I was flattered no end. But as days went by, I felt sad that such a book was going to be published in America and England. Couldn't we imagine a similar publication in France?

I became so obsessed with the idea that, back in Paris, I discussed it with Otis Lebert, the owner of the restaurant Le Taxi Jaune opposite my apartment in the Marais district. By dint of comparing recipes, we had become friends. On my initiative, we decided to write a book of recipes together. After a series of long and heated discussions, we invited Laurent Laffont, my editor, for lunch in order to inform him of our project. I was convinced I could easily win his approval since our friendship dated back to when I published my first novels with Robert Laffont, his father. He had welcomed me with open arms when I indicated I would like to be on the authors' list of the publishing house he had just taken over with his sister. To my great surprise, Laurent gave a categorical refusal. Not only did he have no interest in the project but also, according to him, cookbooks belonged to a specialized field of publishing and distribution. He was so adamant that there was no point insisting. Although Otis accepted his decision somewhat indifferently, I was so disappointed that it forced me to think about the meaningful role cooking had played throughout my life. Together with literature, it had been my dominant passion for years.

Of course both passions are not fully comparable. Cooking goes back to man's animal origins and there's no use elaborating complicated recipes in order to mask this truth. Preparing food does not fall within the domain of the so-called noble occupations, such as mixing colours for a painting or devising rhymes. Yet, very quickly, I realized that both passions could not be radically dissociated. They discreetly share common ground. My taste for cooking therefore was mainly inspired by my desire not to conform to the picture of the perfect little girl, so dear to my parents, especially my mother. Instead of massacring *Letter to Elise* in front of an audience of friends feigning admiration, I preferred the realm of the kitchen. It was the same inclination to displease which accompanied my first attempts at writing. My book *Victoire, My Mother's Mother*, intended to rehabilitate my grandmother, cook to a family of white Creoles, includes a great deal of provocation which is a dominant feature of my personality. As a rule, people are said to be proud to count as an ancestor a poet, a philosopher, a historian whose lost notes they found in a trunk in the attic, or a brave soldier who died for their homeland. To claim as one's own a *dèyè chez*, a servant who never knew how to speak French, smacks of heresy.

Let us delve deeper. I remember how surprised my guests looked as they licked their lips after savouring a capon stuffed with candied fruit or a butterflied sea bass garnished with a pea puree. To be considered an excellent cook also helped me change my image as the militant feminist intellectual I was too often stuck with.

One summer I taught a course at the School of Critical Theory at Cornell University, the ultimate in scholarship where professors of outstanding merit compete for an invitation. While lunching in the dining room, a young African girl dressed in white overalls flung her arms around my neck and reminded me that I used to know her as a child. She was the daughter of two friends in Dakar—her parents ranked among Senegal's most prominent intellectuals, well-known opponents to Léopold Sédar Senghor's government.

'What on earth are you doing here?' I asked her once the effusion had been vented.

'I'm a student at the school for hotel manage-ment,' she explained proudly. 'It's one of the best in the States, you know.'

I did know. My parents would never have let me go in that direction. But what about me? Would I have let my daughters become chefs and not lawyers and economists? On a more personal level, Richard, my husband, is my translator. He examines my books with a critical eye and assails me with questions to clarify his work. His finicky interrogations never stop. But for my talent as a cook—that's a different story. The way to a man's heart is through his stomach, goes the saying. Although there is certainly more at stake between Richard and I than the mere matter of a stomach, it is nevertheless true that a meal together is a moment for relaxing and communicating. When he, educated in the English manner and sparing of compliments, tastes one of my dishes and congratu-lates me, I am filled with plenitude. As I am when my children seated around me at table do justice to my cooking.

'You know full well,' Sylvie, one of my daugh-ters, said recently. 'When we come for dinner, we eat everything in sight.'

'We gobble everything up,' Aïcha, another of my daughters, grins, harking back to her childhood vocabulary.

Yet, all things considered, this feeling of satisfaction after having sated those we love is somewhat banal. After all, woman nurtures.

There is, however, one last consideration I must address with a certain caution as it is perhaps deeper than the others: Does cooking even the score with writing? For me who has such difficulty fitting into Guadeloupean, African and finally African American literature, I who have known so many refusals and exclusions, isn't cooking an easier way to whet the appetite?

When I welcome my guests for the first time, around my table laid with considerable effect with the Chinese Rose Spode dinner service inherited from Marjorie, my mother-in-law, I inevitably venture the same joke: 'I know you'll love it! I'm not sure I'm a good novelist, but I'm convinced I'm a great cook!' Nobody laughs. Not one. It's because my guests are shocked. What sacrilege! they think. How can she be so bold as to compare cooking with literature? It boils down to mixing sheep with goats, jute with silk.

My enduring crime of treason is the subject of this book.

The Apprentice Years:
From Flankoko to Plum Pudding

My childhood leaves me with nothing but bitter-sweet memories. With the sensitivity of a tormented soul, my life transformed the slightest joke, the faintest sarcasm or the most innocent pun into an inconsolable assault. The outside world scared me and I saw hidden dangers everywhere. I had the same dream several times a week: I would leave home to go and buy some sweets and coconut cookies at Amie Rose's, a pastry cook who lived two or three streets away. I would tiptoe out, since my mother had forbidden those candies, claiming they spoilt my teeth. If I insisted on eating them, my smile would reveal a row of blackish stumps. That thought, how-ever, did not prevent me from disobeying her. But no sooner had I set foot outside than I saw to my terror that the surroundings had changed. The familiar upstairs-downstairs houses had disappeared. The street had been transformed into a wasteland lined with rigid, threatening electricity poles. Rows of birds perched on the wires and glared at me, a scene I saw later in a Hitchcock film. Suddenly, monkey-headed monsters surged up out of the ground and hurled themselves onto me, until I was left on the ground, lying in a pool of blood.

The education I received was not likely to make things easier. Although my father paid no attention to me, my mother wrapped me in a finicky, demanding affection that she never had for my seven brothers and sisters. It was precisely this affection which made her too demanding—and made me unable to ever find favour in her eyes. I was too tall, my skin was lacklustre, my eyes were too tiny, my hair too frizzy. I came first in French composition and recitation (which should have made her proud)—but last in maths. I still remember my tears, week after week, as she signed my report card studded with zeros. It was therefore inevitable that I sought refuge in the company of the servants who, unlike my mother, treated me as their little darling.

Two of them stayed in our service for many years. One was Julie, an elegant mulatto woman, around sixty, with wrinkled cheeks and always in a black-and-white checked dress and a black head-tie. What secret love was she mourning? It was rumoured that when she was young, she had been the mistress of a French man who worked for the administration. He had promised to take her to France and marry her. But he hadn't kept his word, and abandoned her on the island. Julie doted on me with all the generosity of her heart. Responsible for taking care of me, she would wash me, dress me, comb my frizzy hair, tie it with pink or blue satin bows, walk me to school and carry my heavy satchel stuffed with exercise books and manuals. On Thursdays, since there was no school, no lessons to be learnt or homework to be done, she accompanied me to the Place de la Victoire and never failed to buy me a snowball (pronounced *sinobol*, and which I discovered years later in Spain as granizados). I was especially fond of the red grenadine, and the white barley water which made my lips deliciously sticky.

'You are the Good Lord's little darling,' she would say over and over, smothering me with kisses.

Unfortunately, she used to go home at 6.30 p.m. and I would be alone again, confronting the terrors of the night.

The other servant was very different. Her name was Adélia, a stout, black, almost blue, woman from Marie-Galante, like my mother. She had a daughter about my age called Michelle who I loved perhaps even more than my sisters. I used to help with her homework, as she was not very clever at school. Michelle cried all the time since her mother's favourite pastime was to knock her about and ill-treat her. I never understood why, and wondered whether a mother's job was not to constantly test her daughter.

I had never thought of sleeping on the second floor where my brothers and sisters slept. I slept, instead, on the first floor, next to my parent's bedroom, in a tiny, austere room where my grandmother Victoire had lived bedridden until her death. Oddly enough, I, who am easily frightened, was not afraid of this deceased grandmother I had never met. Quite the contrary. Her gentle presence comforted me during my long sleepless hours. Having my parents close by was not that reassuring. I could hear them murmuring. I could hear their heavy steps as they got out of bed to relieve themselves noisily in the water closet. The nights were always never-ending and I longed for the morning.

In the lovely house we lived in on the rue Alexandre Isaac, my favourite refuge was the kitchen. I would dash in whenever Julie, who used to do the washing, was occupied elsewhere. It was a terribly untidy place. The pool of clean water in the middle overflowed with dirty plates left to soak. Dishes, saucepans, pots and pans lay on the tiled floor. The shelves were full of jars containing a mixture of sundry spices: saffron, nutmeg, cinnamon, hot peppers, black pepper, chervil, marjoram and bay rum leaves. A cavern of Ali Baba, a concoction of scents.

Adélia used to let me season the meat and the fish.

'I can't understand you,' she'd grumble. 'You're the first in your class but all you're interested in is poking your nose in the kitchen.'

Already inventive, I suggested replacing the potatoes in a cod brandade with sweet potatoes or yams.

'You must be joking,' she laughed.

One day she let me make the flankoko for dessert. I carefully mixed the water, condensed milk, flour and powdered coconut. But when I decided to add two spoonfuls of aged rum, Adélia was adamant: 'You don't put aged rum in a flan!'

Adélia announced to the family that night that the flan was entirely my doing. During the week, eating was more a question of quantity than quality. My seven brothers and sisters as well as my father would wolf down the pork stew, red beans, rice and yams that Adélia routinely cooked. She reserved her ingenuity for Sunday lunch and birthdays when she would cook to perfection crab dumplings, casserole of red tuna and curried goat. That very evening, on a full stomach, the family complimented me politely but without conviction. My mother even blurted out: 'Only stupid people like to cook.'

Did she really say that? Or was it my imagination, because her irrevocable condemnation fitted her character? I cannot say for sure. Whatever the case, her cruel, unfair and rather stupid declaration has never stopped repeating itself in my mind.

In my book *Victoire, My Mother's Mother*, I venture an explication by describing my mother's complex feelings towards her own mother, an excellent cook, totally illiterate, who was hired by a family of white Creoles.

That same evening, I did not follow my brothers and sisters up to the second floor. I could hear them laugh, talk in Creole and play the guitar until my father told them it was time to go to bed. He'd thump the ceiling with a broom stick and shout: 'Lights out, children!'

I locked myself in my room and cried the whole night through. But it didn't prevent me from helping out Adélia. On the contrary, it made me defiant. I would skilfully flour the blue and pink parrot fish in order to barbecue them. However much Adélia, who was devilishly traditional, protested, I concocted pink grapefruit and avocado salads, copiously seasoned with lemon juice. From that moment on, every time I stepped into the kitchen I felt I was defying a taboo or breaking a law, a sensation I felt again years later when I started to kiss boys on the mouth like in the movies. At the age of fifteen, I was capable of cooking a Colombo of curried goat, the national dish we inherited from the Indians. However, I never managed to get Adélia's approval. She'd purse her lips in disapproval: 'Why on earth did you add powdered cinnamon? Cinnamon has no place in a Colombo!'

Why not? Who decided that? I was not in favour of the traditional dishes whose unchanging recipes seem to come from sacred texts inherited from our ancestors. I liked to create and invent. Although Adélia did not appreciate my inventions, the same wasn't true for Michelle who loved my cooking. One day, I had the idea of mixing pork, crab meat and spinach shoots. Adélia was scandalized and refused to taste the horrible mixture: 'What kind of pig's swill is that?'

Michelle and I, however, stuffed ourselves, and Michelle went so far as to declare she had never tasted anything so good in her life.

Unfortunately, Julie and Adélia both passed out of my life around the same time. In *Tales from the Heart: True Stories from My Childhood*, I describe the shock I felt at witnessing the first brutal loss of a loved one. One morning, Julie did not turn up for work, so one of my sisters had to take me to school. Since there was no sign of her at noon, one of my brothers was sent to enquire after her. He found the neighbourhood plunged in grief. The evening before, hardly had she put her key in the lock than she collapsed on the ground: snuffed out like a candle. Heart attack.

Shortly afterwards, Adélia and my mother quarrelled (again). This time Adélia was asking for a raise since she was working too hard, doing the shopping *and* the cooking. There were ten of us to be fed twice a day. She would arrive at six in the morning and there was no rule as to when she could go back home to the other side of town. But my mother refused, so the two women went their separate ways. Adélia went back to Marie-Galante where she opened a restaurant called *A La Chaubette Gourmande* (The Hungry Clam). I could imagine it very well, as I knew it was located in Saint-Louis, not far from the pier. The shack was sturdy but rundown under its red corrugated-iron roof. Adélia's skills as a cook attracted a good number of customers who would dig into the fish blaff, sucking noisily on the bones. Sometimes a brawl would break out but was soon settled over glasses of 65 proof Père Labat rum.

Adélia was replaced by a stout, high, yellow woman from the suburbs. Every time I poked my nose in the kitchen, she shouted: 'What are you doing here? Get out!'

My passion for cooking went hand in hand with my dream for freedom. This attraction was an innate part of my personality. Why did my mother want to hurt me? Why did she want to stifle it?

In 1951, I passed my baccalaureate and left to study classics in Paris. The Atlantic crossing on the *Katoomba* which would take us to Le Havre to catch the maritime train, commonly known as the 'the Negro Train', introduced me to a new-found taste of freedom. I could wake up and go to bed whenever I wanted, I could refuse to eat the thick, creamy yoghurts I loathed, attend the shows I liked and flirt with whomever I pleased. Unfortunately, apart from two or three idiots, hardly any boy paid me attention. In order to attract these malingering males, I was tempted to simper and smile and feign a pose but found it all too humiliating.

My feelings on leaving my native island were not simple. I had been scolded too much by my mother and forced to live in a closed social circle. And yet I missed that protection. My dread of others made me fear the worst. What did the future have in store for me? What was it hiding beyond the white caps of the ocean? At the end of the crossing, I feverishly jotted down the address of Josette who had shared my cabin and was off to study law in Bordeaux. We promised to write to each other but never did.

The arrival of the 'Negro Train' at the Saint-Lazare railway station was a highly colourful event, no pun intended. Those passengers arriving from Guadeloupe, Martinique and French Guiana had dressed up to the nines. Unfortunately they committed some obvious faux-pas: the women wore stockings two shades too light and were overloaded with jewels; the men wore ill-fitting jackets that visibly indicated they were new arrivals. They were greeted by families who had settled in Paris thanks to the BUMIDOM (an agency for recruiting overseas workers) and whom, very often, they hadn't seen in years. A cacophony of cries of joy and recognition as well as exclamations and kissing. The new arrivals were especially smitten with the children born during their separation: '*A pa jé, non*! You'd think they're little white children the way they speak!'

As for me, my sisters Ena and Gilette were waiting for me since my brother, Sandrino, had begun his slow death at the hospital in Berck; the doctors were convinced he was suffering from a bone disease. Ena was wearing a large black astrakhan coat although we were only in early September. She inspected me from head to toe and finally said: 'You're a grown girl now. Be extra careful, Paris is full of unscrupulous boys.'

She didn't realize how true this was.

My sisters took me to Germaine's, a fellow islander who owned a restaurant on the rue André-Antoine. My first dinner in Paris therefore was Guadeloupean: cod fritters, curried chicken Colombo,

Creole rice and the inevitable coconut flan as a dessert. I was delighted since at that time France was the realm of indigestible dishes such as cauliflower cheese, mashed potatoes and braised endives.

I had been selected by the prestigious Lycée Fénélon to sit for the entrance exam to the Ecole normale supérieure. Typical of that time, we were only two black students in the preparatory classes, Marguerite Senghor from Senegal and I. Perhaps because of that, in order to pass unseen, there was never any contact between the two of us. We ignored each other.

I lived on the rue Lhomond. On weekdays, I had to be content with the tasteless meals served at the respectable Pierre de Coubertin hostel where I was a boarder: boiled potatoes, every kind of cabbage imaginable, green cabbage, red cabbage, cauliflower and Brussels sprouts, invariably overcooked, and nondescript fish fingers. The weekends I spent at my sisters'. One of them, also my godmother, lived in an exquisite apartment on Place des Abbesses and never failed to serve for lunch a horse steak garnished with fries. I ate it alone in the kitchen while she played Chopin waltzes to perfection in her bedroom. That was when horse butchers enjoyed enormous success and displayed outside their shops gilded metal signs of a giant horse's head. But the smell I associated with them made me feel sick. As a result, I had great difficulty swallowing what was put in front of me.

My other sister lived at the Carrefour Pleyel in Saint-Denis. She toiled hard as a social worker in that underprivileged suburb and by the weekend was exhausted and hardly in the mood for cooking. She fed her daughter jars of baby food which had begun to go on sale in the pharmacies and supermarkets. As for her husband: she dished him up roast chicken from the neighbourhood caterer. Caterer is a fancy word for the modest store that sold cooked meat and vegetables. He would wolf down two mouthfuls, push his plate aside and disappear on his motorbike. 'Where is he off to?' my sister would wonder bitterly. We learnt later that he was courting a wishy-washy fair-headed girl, a nurse by trade who lived with her parents at the Porte de Clignancourt; he had even asked for her hand. (When the truth came out, my sister threatened to divorce.) I was convinced he had surrendered to the appeal of French cuisine.

In fact, since I was often invited by my class-mates for Sunday lunch, I discovered to my surprise that France was a place where you could eat well, have a feast, and that tourists came from far and wide to eat foie gras, rabbit cooked in prunes and sweetbreads.

After having almost lost her husband, my sister went to work in the kitchen. But since her heart was not in it, she would overcook her roasts and burn her quiches and pizzas to a cinder. I offered to help her. Amazed, she watched me stick the roast meat with garlic and cloves or macerate breasts of chicken in aged rum and raisins.

'Who taught you all that?' she asked.

'Nobody,' I answered. 'It came to me in a dream.'

'Nonsense! You have to learn to cook.'

No. The art of cooking is a gift. Like all the other gifts, nobody knows where it comes from.

During that same period, I discovered the joys of travel, I who had never left Guadeloupe, not even to go to Martinique. I soon realized that a foreign country cannot be differentiated merely by its literature or music—a foreign country amounts first and foremost to its cuisine. At school, exasperated by our terrible accents, our teachers had introduced us to Shakespeare. But England does not boil down to Hamlet, Macbeth or Othello—it's also the land of the leg of lamb with mint sauce, of fish and chips sold in greasy newspaper, soaked in vinegar, and that nobody told us about. A country's cuisine mirrors the character of its inhabitants and transfigures the imagination. Visiting a supermarket is as instructive as going to a museum or an exhibition. Like all students my age, I often went to England, to Kent in particular. At that time, the journey was endless: you had to take the train at the Gare du Nord in Paris, then the ferry to cross the Channel and admire the white cliffs of Dover. Sitting by the window in the smoking room, I looked out at the dull, grey sea which had nothing in common with the one I knew in Guadeloupe, and was amazed that the same word could even be applied to such different elements while the seagulls hovered over the ship uttering lugubrious cries.

I was a guest of the Coopers, a nice family who lived in the moribund town of Folkestone. Mr Cooper worked as a police superintendent but ran a theatre club. His elder son made himself up as Othello, the Moor of Venice, while the younger one played Iago. I was regularly assigned the role of one of the three witches in *Macbeth*. I was too young and too innocent to detect his underlying racism and rebel against the comparison of a black woman with a witch. At the same time I was piqued as I dreamt of playing Lady Macbeth, a role he reserved for his eldest daughter, a blonde with greenish-blue eyes.

Mrs Cooper was surprised at my interest in English cuisine which at the time had a bad reputation.

'There's no need to season vegetables,' she recommended. 'Our vegetables are so tasty, the slightest spice would spoil them. And you shouldn't cook them too long.'

I reluctantly obeyed and let the peas roll around together and the carrots and turnips crunch at first bite. Mrs Cooper paid me an honour of the highest order by giving me the recipe for a Christmas pudding, delicately prepared with crystallized fruit carefully macerated in exact quantities of alcohol.

Back in Paris I aroused my sister's curiosity by replacing the traditional Yule log on Christmas Eve by a surprise of my own invention. It turned out to be a great success. But I don't know whether Mrs Cooper would have approved as I replaced the sultanas with slivers of candied dates. My sister couldn't get over it.

'Where did you learn all that?' she asked.

I proudly gave an explanation. But cooking was decidedly out of favour with the family as my other sister, who was present, shrugged and said mockingly: 'We thought you went to England to learn English. It turns out you went to learn how to make cakes.'

One year, I renounced my routine and travelled to Italy whose cultural treasures and museums were constantly extolled by my teachers. Much to my surprise, I took a dislike to it instantly because of the awful pasta which was the main item on every menu and served up meal after meal. In Florence, moreover, it was stifling hot. Then I had to line up for an hour to gain admittance to the Uffizi Gallery where I coldly contemplated Botticelli's *Birth of Venus*. The young woman was pretty skinny and not that lovely. I swore never to set foot in Italy again and almost kept my word since it was another twenty years or so before I returned after taking a liking to Canaletto's paintings.

I visited Spain on several occasions. But my favourite was Portugal. The men were dark-skinned like mulattos. Their gleaming white smiles broke a hole in their faces. They would follow the girls along the beach, admiring their swimsuits and shouting flattering names. It did me a lot of good as I believed myself to be ill-favoured by Nature. Furthermore, the *bacalao* of my childhood was omnipresent, dressed in a fashion that would certainly have displeased

Adélia. I often returned to Albufeira and Faro where, in the small seaside cafes, I ate grilled sardines in the company of handsome Portuguese men whose advances I pretended to ignore.

In June 1955, I went on a journey of a totally different type—I travelled to the World Festival of Youth and Students in Warsaw. I had never been to any Eastern European country and was dying to know what Poland had in store for me. There were also other considerations to take into account, ideological ones. I had begun to have political opinions. I used to go to meetings of Young Communists on the rue Saint-André-des-Arts where a professor with hair down to his shoulders explained the philosophy of Karl Marx. The prominent Marxist historians, Jean-Suret Canale and Jean Bruhat, taught me the surprising fact that I was colonized. The language I had spoken since childhood, the religion my mother had inculcated me with and the habit I was wearing, they said, were all borrowed. The truth lay elsewhere. All that was highly complex. I was like a child who suddenly finds out she is adopted. What kind of attitude should I take with my biological parents? Even more painful, Suret-Canale and Bruhat told me that Portugal, the country I adored, had been the forerunner of a loathsome colonial expansion. Its priests and missionaries had disfigured Brazil and made the Tupi Indians into savages. Fortunately, they reassured me, countries always end up throwing off the colonial yoke. Brazil had become independent and soon it would be the turn of Mozambique and Angola, Portugal's African possessions.

In Warsaw, our delegation, pompously named 'Delegation from the African Diaspora', was housed in the brand-new suburb of Nova Huta. When we went out to visit the town, we were assailed by men, women and children, all inevitably white with blue eyes, who touched our hair and stroked our cheeks to see if our colour would rub off. It reminded me of the poem by Nicolas Guillen: 'It was all a question of cheap colours, none of which was stable.' The Poles who surrounded us were not aggressive, merely curious. Yet their attitude was disagreeable and made us feel like aliens. The next day, the festival's opening procession lasted four hours. Although the African Diaspora delegation amounted to scarcely a dozen boys and girls, mostly from Haïti, the other countries were represented in great numbers. I saw Japanese, Chinese, Indians and Pakistanis, dressed in their finest national costumes, marching past. I was especially fascinated by the Mongols with their large square faces and slit eyes. I enquired about their history and learnt that they were once fierce warriors on horseback and that one of their leaders was called Genghis Khan. The meal that was to follow and unite us in the monumental festival hall was, alas, not up to the event: the winsome blond-haired and blue-eyed waiters brought in dishes loaded only with boiled potatoes and sausages. Was that the Pole's usual fare? Was that the best they could give to their visitors?

The festival lasted a week and offered a series of competitive sports, concerts, ballets, operas and plays of which I didn't understand a word but whose splendour dazzled me. Unfortunately, the meals were all the same. I was filled with dismay. Even the day before we left, when a solemn circular invited us to a farewell banquet in the festival hall, it was the same. The only difference: an appetizer of thick soup in which chunks of meat collided with carrots and potatoes.

I returned to Paris my head buzzing with questions. Was it possible to satisfy the soul with so many marvels, so many cultural treasures but to leave the body unsatisfied and hungry for more? Is spiritual munificence enough to compensate physical inadequacy? It wasn't only Poland's cultural treasures but also those of its allies linked by the thread of ideology. Poland had merely known how to display and organize them. But doesn't a country's cuisine and culture depend also on its socioeconomic conditions? Wasn't I wrong not to take those into account? Little Poland, hemmed in, trampled by the boots of the German and Russian ruffians, was perhaps, above all, rich with suffering. I was soon to find out that the incompetence of leaders and dictators would certainly have negative effects.

THE MULTIPLE VARIATIONS OF MAFÉ

In *What Is Africa to Me?*, an unsentimental auto-biography, I wrote in detail about the leaden years I went through before becoming a writer. I have no intention whatsoever of repeating myself here. So I shall merely say that, during the years I spent in Guinea, eating was reduced to its purely physical function: filling one's stomach in order to survive. Moreover, there wasn't a single restaurant in Conakry besides the one at the hotel in Camayenne (which served 'continental' cuisine without ever indicating what continent it was referring to). Sometimes, around the edge of the bus stations, the market women managed to procure some plantains, sell kelewele or aloko. I left the cooking in the hands of my boy, Ibrahima, a Peul with a famished expression which did not augur well. Appearances, however, are deceiving. He spent most of his time scouring the markets in search of food. Whenever he was lucky enough to unearth a chicken as big as your fist or a tough, stony chunk of meat, we'd celebrate. I would bring out the silverware, a wedding present from one of my sisters, and invite Françoise, a friend from

Guadeloupe who lived three houses down. She had taken advantage of her holiday in Sainte-Anne to bring back a stock of salted codfish, so as least she could make accras or cod fritters.

Ibrahima invariably cooked a mafé. Mafé is a dish from Mali very easy to prepare as it only requires meat, peanut paste and tomato sauce. You can also add cabbage and sweet potatoes but that, given our impoverished state, seldom happened. I loved mafé. And it did not require palm oil. (Long before today's dieticians, I loathed this condiment; I considered it too greasy as well as dangerous for one's health.) Consequently, the mere mention of mafé conjures up for me food shortages and a country's destitution. I had little idea that one day it would turn out to give me a delicious surprise.

No sooner had I settled down in Winneba in Ghana where I taught French than I was invited to a literary afternoon in Accra. It meant a drive back into town, 60 kilometres along a dangerous road busy with large trucks. Yet I didn't hesitate for a moment. It had been too long since I had attended a meeting for intellectuals. I was going soft in the head. To think that at the age of twenty I was capable of holding forth with brio on sticky topics such as 'Can the pursuit of happiness justify an entire life?' For the time being, I had trouble helping my children do their homework!

I therefore headed enthusiastically for the Mahatma Gandhi Hall on the University of Ghana campus at Legon, a grandiose, imposing edifice built by Kwame NKrumah. I was the only person dressed as a European in the midst of a riot of flowing embroidered boubous and gigantic head ties. The crowd seemed oddly debonair to me since I had lost the habit of being around joyful convivial smiles. The speaker was a writer by the name of George Awoonor-Williams. Little did we know that he would be assassinated by terrorists during the 2013 Westgate massacre in Nairobi. He explained that, henceforth, he was to be called Kofi Awoonor; to rid himself of the English aspects of his name was an act of faith. He insisted on the debt we owed to Africa and the need to rehabilitate her. The discussion that followed was lively. I noticed a young writer, Ayi Kwei Armah, whom I was to meet again years later in the US during his never-ending exile. Regimes came and went and nobody wanted him. At the time he was hot-headed and determined. He would repeat: 'Do not be afraid, above all don't be afraid of those who govern us.'

Once the discussion was over, Kofi Awoonor came over and kindly invited me to dinner. I was dumbfounded, since I was neither a writer nor journalist. The honour he paid me was probably due to my status as a foreigner from a place so far away. So I headed out with the group of guests, full of the wonderful feeling of resuming my seat in the family of humans.

Beyond the gates of the university, Accra was a lively mixture of noise and disorder. Strains of high

life sounded all around us. Passing in front of a gar-
ishly illuminated house, its doors and windows flung
open, the voice of a singer rang out, repeating the
popular refrain: 'Akepete-shi is no good, oh! No
good, oh!' I never liked Accra, and always thought
its bustle rather vulgar. Yet there was something
pleasant about walking through the noise of the night
with that warm-hearted company after being
deprived for so long of intellectual nourishment. The
restaurant was called A la Reine Pokou and, to tell
the truth, wasn't much to look at. Waitresses with
outrageously straightened red hair, their breasts and
buttocks spilling out of their uniforms, rushed about,
their arms loaded with dishes. I looked at the menu—
and to my amazement the speciality was mafé! A
waitress set down a plate in front of me. Besides the
mutton, I recognized smoked fish, snails, small crabs,
spinach and a variety of bitter greens called agu.
Agathe, the owner, joined us since she was the mistress of one of the professors. She was a very pretty
woman despite an ugly wig. She sat down beside me
and told me she was French-speaking, originally from
the Ivory Coast.

'I have never tasted such a wonderful mafé!' I
exclaimed warmly.

'It's because my cook prepares it in the Ashanti
manner,' she replied. 'I don't know how she does it.
And yet I'm Baoulé, the same people, you know.'

I did know. Of course, I knew about the legend
of Queen Abra Pokou fleeing the Gold Coast, forced

to cross a river with her suite. When, amid the tumult, her son drowned, she had moaned '*Baoulé*'—'My son is dead'. That's how she gave the name to an ethnic group which was to flourish in Ivory Coast. Once again I was deeply impressed by how the language we speak (even if it is 'borrowed', as my intellectual masters claimed) draws people closer. Because we shared the same French language, Agathe and I felt we had known each other for years. We began to chat, oblivious of the general conversation. She confided that the university at Legon was a hotbed of anti-establishment opponents to Kwame NKrumah's regime. Her partner wrote inflammatory articles in the university journal. As a result, she dreamt of taking him away to the Ivory Coast where he would be safe.

'At least Houphouët-Boigny doesn't put people in prison.'

'I can't understand this opposition,' I murmured, disconcerted. 'It's surely better than when the British were here.'

'Perhaps,' she sighed. 'But it's far from what we dreamt of.'

'Far from what we dreamt of?' But weren't we naive to imagine that in next to no time our peoples would be educated, clothed, housed and happy? Independence was a terrible purgatory with the promise of happiness.

On parting we exchanged addresses. When she heard that I lived in Winneba she exclaimed: 'Have you heard of Pedro Leal? He owns a restaurant on the beach where they serve great food, especially an excellent mafé.'

I promised her I would check him out. But there were my numerous obligations as a mother to take into account and so two or three weeks passed before I had the time. A former fishing village, Winneba was not a very pleasant place. It was poorly lit and the streets were furrowed with ruts and strewn with garbage. Half a dozen shacks were strung out along a beach cluttered with seaweed and objects of every sort—bicycles without handlebars, barrels of oil and even the skeleton of a jeep without wheels. All the shacks housed restaurants, and Pedro Leal's was called Saudade. Like all the others, it was nothing to look at. Poorly lit, four or five rickety tables looking out onto a black sea which collided with a sky streaked with yellow. Not a single customer. Pedro Leal was a tall, lanky black guy whose age was difficult to guess despite a resolutely white mop of hair.

'I'm sure you'll love my mafé,' he exclaimed, pleased with himself.

We sat down at table laid with glasses of the local alcohol.

'I'm from Guinea-Bissau. For twenty years I was a steward in the merchant navy on a route from Bissau to Recife in Brazil. I was treated like a dog by those Portuguese swine. Can you imagine, I caught pneumonia and almost died. But they didn't think twice about kicking me out without a cent. I was incapable of looking after myself. I was lucky in my misfortune and got to know a woman, a Ga, from here. Her country, Ghana, had just won its independence and was trying to offer a new life for Africans. Everything was free. She admitted me to the Korle Bu Hospital. Unfortunately she died from a dengue fever she caught I don't know where. After a few months, I moved here to Winneba. I missed her and the ocean so much, I couldn't get over either of them. The pain has subsided a bit. I cook all my mother's recipes here. I never paid any attention when she used to do the cooking: it's not a boy's place. Suddenly, it all came back to me.'

At that moment the waitress brought me my dish of mafé: a real delight but radically different from the one I had tasted at the Reine Pokou. No smoked fish or shellfish but seasoned with tamarind and spiced with aniseed.

I often returned to Pedro Leal's restaurant, not only for the mafé but also to listen to his stories which invariably tore the Portuguese to pieces.

'Lisbon is a terrible place. If you collapse in the street, the cars will run over you and nobody will bother to find out what happened. I lived there for a year, unemployed, trafficking drugs to survive like everyone else: cocaine, heroin, marijuana, anything goes.'

I also loved listening to him talk of the ocean. Twice a day, braving the reef and the currents, he would slip on his black Lycra swimsuit, dive into the sea and head out towards the horizon. Soon, all you could see of him was his white hair foaming above the green waters. Then he would swim back to the beach and fall on the sand to dry in the sun. The ocean, he told me, was a mistress you never tired of. You never felt like cheating on her. She possessed you entirely.

One evening, I took two Togolese, M. and Mme Theoda, my only friends in Winneba, to dinner at the restaurant. They were parents to six adorable little girls who got on very well with mine. M. Theoda taught revolutionary filmography. I never knew what that meant and I never attended any of his projections in the Institute's huge cinema. He was no bigger than his oldest daughter aged ten. Yet that fragile little man had been accused of having a hand in the assassination of President Sylvanus Olympio. He had escaped with his life thanks only to the incredible help from his friends in the opposition. He strongly denied committing such a crime but I only half believed him. An uncompromising idealist who could justify any kind of excess, he was particularly sad that day and downed four glasses of white wine one after the other.

'I have just received news of my mother,' he lamented, his eyelids drooping over his protruding eyes and tears rolling down his cheeks. 'My cousin called. She fell in our courtyard and broke her leg. She's got to spend three months in plaster and now I won't be there beside her when she dies.'

Used to his fits of depression, his wife, a matronly woman, scolded: 'Enough of this nonsense. You know full well that Grunitzky's government is on the verge of collapse, and we'll soon be able to go home.'

Then, barely swallowing two mouthfuls from her plate, she exclaimed: 'That's not a mafé! I'll invite you to our place and you'll see what a *real* mafé tastes like!'

Those uncompromising words reminded me of Adélia's. Real? Wrong? What does that mean?

Going from what I had just experienced, I concluded that a dish, any dish, varied according to who prepared it. Mafé was based on a common recipe of groundnuts, tomato sauce and meat; therafter, all sorts of modifications were permitted. Cooking is an art. It relies on an individual's fantasy, invention and freedom. Cookbooks are for dummies. There are no such things as rules and directives.

The following week, the Theodas invited me for dinner, and Mme Theoda served up a plain mafé. Her husband, a heavy drinker, had concocted a cocktail with coconut milk, Cinzano and a very expensive blue gin you needed to pay foreign currency for. I was knocked out with my very first glass.

M. Theoda was overjoyed because the university was on strike. 'Africa doesn't need universities,' he repeated in his high-pitched voice. 'What we need is professional training where our youth learn the techniques to put an end to our backwardness.'

'Be a little more ambitious,' said his wife who loved to contradict him. 'In the sixteenth century, we already had prestigious universities.'

M. Theoda shrugged: 'Sankoré! I know, I know! Nevertheless, we've never been able to make a darned nail or bolt.'

'Those who have invented neither gunpowder nor compass': Aimé Césaire's verse echoed in my memory but, given my drunken state, I was unable to say a word.

My time in Ghana, however, didn't boil down to tracking down the different places where they cooked mafé. Nevertheless a final anecdote comes to mind. When I returned to Accra to work, in the evenings, deafened by my children's squabbling, I would get out for dinner to the Akwapim district, a neighbourhood close to mine and populated by immigrants of every nationality. There must have been a large number from the Sahel, since the sounds of the kora and balafon could be heard through the open windows. Memory is totally illogical. These sounds filled me with a nostalgia which I found irritating. Was I going to regret Guinea where I had led such a lifeless existence and dreamt so many times of escaping? In spite of my anger, however, there emerged the memory of the faces of the men and women I had met and my eyes brimmed with tears.

I was especially fond of the Moro-Naba. They made an excellent mafé, a little like Ibrahima's but garnished with different vegetables and even cassava.

The Moro-Naba belonged to two natives of Burkino Faso, then called Upper Volta. Issifou the husband, a handsome man, would emerge around eleven in the evening, wearing a heavy double-breasted suit which would have looked well on a trader in the City of London. Yaba, his wife, sat imposingly behind the cash register. In a way, Issifou and Yaba had succeeded. He had managed to be hired as a municipal gardener in a team who mowed and raked all day long the town's many lawns. She owned this restaurant which was always packed with customers. On my third or fourth visit, she hauled herself out from behind the desk, came over to my table and, breathing heavily, said: 'So you haven't got a husband!'

I could have replied that I had two, one legitimate and another, but I merely answered in the negative. Yaba immediately sat down in front of me. Her eyes narrowed. 'You're right. Our men are good for nothing. Issifou wants a divorce to marry a Fanti woman he met here. He says I haven't produced a single child during the fourteen years we've been together. I'm of no use. All I do is spend his money. But he won't get me out of here. If he makes trouble, I'll complain to the local committee and then he'll see what happens. Here you don't treat women like at home.'

Ghana, it's true, could be proud of its social-welfare policy which was unique to Africa. Lawyers, social workers and consultants offered all kinds of free advice in the offices of the neighbourhood committees.

'I do hope your problems manage to be settled,' I said to Yaba. 'And that you manage to keep your restaurant.'

'I'll keep it, Inshallah!' she assured me with a laugh.

Despite her outward display of assurance, the next time I went back to the Moro-Naba, Yaba had disappeared. Behind the cash desk sat a young Ghanaian girl, very obviously pregnant. Apparently, Issifou had had the last word.

I recently discovered a cardboard box containing some old bills, some poor snapshots of my children, and, much to my surprise, two nicely printed menus for 'Dinner on April 24th at Maryse Condé's'. What was this date? It was neither my birthday nor none of my children's. Who had I invited to this dinner, I who knew hardly anyone in Accra? Why had I had these menus printed? . . . I do recall how I was suddenly overcome with an enthusiasm which forced me out of the closet like a homosexual who decides to reveal his sexual orientation. Perhaps I was tired of being anonymous, a woman without status or appeal. I must have already been burning with a desire to draw attention to myself, blazing with something whose nature I did not understand. I was not yet dreaming of becoming a writer, far from it. But I was ready to give free rein to this other talent, this art of the cuisine. It was only much later and slightly out of fun that I attributed my gift to Victoire, my grandmother, a renowned cook. I had inherited it from her without knowing it or her.

I think I spent two days in the markets, examining and weighing vegetables, checking the lustre of the eyes of the fish and sniffing the freshness of the meat. I finally drew up a menu to my liking: grouper and shrimp consommé; gratin of black and white snail meat; and agouti in a sauce of bitter spinach. I gave up only on dessert and made do with ice cream.

'Yum-yum, that looks delicious,' the printer exclaimed when I took him the menu I intended to hand out to my guests. 'Do you own a restaurant? Where is it?'

'No. I teach French at the Ghana Institute of Languages.'

Much less appealing. The printer lost interest and merely scribbled out a bill.

I locked myself up for an entire day in the kitchen, dismissing Adisa as well as my cook. I remained deaf to the frightened cries of my children who shouted, 'Are you all right, Mummy?' from the other side of the closed door.

That evening, my reputation as a cook was established in the small circle in which we lived. That dinner took on the proportions of a myth. From that moment on, any occasion was a pretext to start again: Ghana's Independence Day, Mother's Day, Valentine's Day . . . To celebrate the tenth birthday of one of my daughters, I invited her entire class for what I called a pink lunch composed of pink papaya, shrimp and salmon. Only the sweet-potato mash was slightly orange. Though that aviary of little girls chirped and frolicked, I sensed that they would have preferred hamburgers, chicken nuggets and fries from the McDonald's that had just opened near Flagstaff House.

When my sister came to spend a few weeks with me, I invited fifteen people, including three couples from the neighbourhood whom I hardly knew. I had said hello a few times and their children went to the same school as mine.

'Why are you going to so much trouble?' my sister wondered. 'Eating is a passing pleasure. Once eaten, there's nothing left.'

'It procures a few moments of happiness,' I replied.

'Happiness? You call that happiness?'

I was convinced it was. If happiness, as we know, is relative, why not take advantage of it?

Cooking changed my character. Although in love I was notoriously monogamous, in cooking I dreamt of sharing, multiplying and giving pleasure and delight to as many guests and strangers as possible. Yet the slightest predicament, the slightest affliction took me away from my kitchen, and, because of the ups and downs of my personal life, I stayed almost three years without cooking.

I can remember every detail of one Christmas Eve, the last I was to spend in Africa, in Kaolack, Senegal, where I had just met Richard, who was to become my husband. It was not the first time I had celebrated Christmas in a Muslim land, and each time I have been amazed at the number of Christians on bended knee in the churches. How much longer would this religious tolerance last, already falling apart in so many places across the globe? Midnight Mass had been brought forward to 8 p.m. because of the climate of insecurity that had begun to prevail across the country, an excellent topic for the sermon by the parish priest, a South American, Colombian I believe. He had urged the parishioners to forsake the violence and turn in unison towards the peace and love of God. When I left church, the night was so dark it seemed I was staring into hell. Not at all a silent, holy night. The patter of the Faithfuls' worn-out shoes made the cats and other nocturnal, perhaps even malevolent, animals scatter far and wide.

For Christmas Eve dinner, we had brought out the dining table onto the balcony and covered it with a white wrapper woven with golden thread. Unfortunately, we were unable to hide the holes and cracks on the corrugated-iron ceiling nor the ugliness of our surroundings. We had been content to hang coloured lanterns instead. Since the Muslim baker had been horrified at the thought of roasting the suckling pig in his oven, I had to cut it up in chunks, steam it and season it with all the candied fruit I could find. Browned just right, crisp, almost caramelized, it turned out perfectly.

This suckling pig also marked the advent of my new life.

You Have to Start Somewhere

When I returned to Paris after twelve years of hardship in Africa, an early winter had set in. The trees in the Luxembourg gardens had lost their leaves and stood silhouetted against the grey sky. The sun seemed to have vanished forever. My mood was especially gloomy since I had to settle in on my own: Richard had gone back to England to sort out a number of problems before coming back to live with me. Added to the pain of separation were a host of difficulties. Since my resources were extremely limited, I rented two furnished rooms in a shabby fourth-floor walk-up in Port-Royal. It looked out onto a tiny garden and its occupants were a motley lot. My neighbour to the right was a Brazilian naïf painter, Waldomiro de Deus, who signed all his works with the silhouette of a small dog. He could not understand my fidelity to someone who was absent: 'Unless you tell him,' he said, 'he'll never know.'

My neighbour to the left was a Martinican girl who had briefly lived in Guinea at the same time as me I. She had been the mistress of the Secretary of

State for Industry whom Sékou Touré in next to no time had sent to languish, and finally perish, in prison. Ever since, she ranted on about the new African leaders: 'They're all dictators! Worse than the colonizers.'

Among the other lodgers was a family of Italians, very fond of Chianti, who quarrelled noisily around midnight; two Poles; and a horde of South Americans who had chosen to live in exile in Paris, including two women from Venezuela, Myriam and Fina. They were not only members of an outlawed left-wing party but also excellent cooks. On Saturdays, they would treat us to pork stew, tuna brochettes and red-pepper puree. They taught me a lot since about Latin America, its bloody dictatorships and the constant political interference by the United States. I was a good student and rapidly swallowed everything they taught me. With Fina and Myriam on either side, I marched from the République to Nation on the death of Salvador Allende; and armed with a dictionary, since my Spanish was extremely rudimentary, I deciphered the essays of Paulo Freire and Gilberto Freyre and the novels of Jorge Amado.

It was during one of their dinners that I made the acquaintance of an Argentinean, Gabriel Garcia Roy, and his wife, Dora. Gabriel was a theatre director. Despite his visible impecuniousness, he managed a small theatre company; it had just produced a play that had got a favourable three-line review on the back page of *Le Monde*. With his hair down to his shoulders—it was the fashion at the time—he had the zeal and the seduction of a bard. He urged me to write for the theatre because, he assured me, the novel was a bourgeois art. Only the theatre immediately connected the author to his public. The playwright became the voice of the voiceless.

I had trouble getting acclimatized to Paris again. I hadn't felt cold for over ten years and had to get used to the drab days, the frost and the ice. In the mornings, I would listen to the weather forecast on my transistor radio and feel like burying my head back under my pillow. Unfortunately, I had to get up, get dressed and then walk, shivering, to a smelly, overcrowded Métro. At the age of forty, I had to resume my studies, writing a thesis in comparative literature under the direction of Professor René Etiemble. If he hadn't been so kind, if he hadn't treated me not like a commonplace student but like a woman whose life's ups and downs had deprived her of intellectual scholarship, I would never have finished my thesis in record time. I chose a subject of minor interest—'Black Stereotypes in Negro-African Literature'—which I thought I could carry off without too much trouble. I was also putting the finishing touches to my novel *Heremakhonon*. I was determined to finish that too, since I thought it important to silence the myths about African independence and publish my personal experience. I had also let myself be won over by Gabriel's flamboyant discourse and begun writing a play: *Le Morne de Massabielle* (The

Hill of Massabielle). Why did I choose this title? What memories did it bring back? I no longer recall . . .

(Massabielle is a popular district of Pointe-à-Pitre, full of modest wooden shacks. At the top of the hill is a church dedicated to the Holy Virgin of the Grand Retour. Around her waist she wears a wide blue ribbon; on 15 August, she is paraded through the town. If the procession was to pass through our street, I helped my mother decorate the front of our house, stack potted plants on our balcony and shower the pavement in front with flower petals. Some people are convinced that the Virgin has enormous powers and that she accomplishes miracles.)

In other words, I was far from idle. I had my reserved seat at the National Library on the rue Richelieu where I was a daily visitor. For lunch, I ate a sandwich and gulped cups of strong coffee. I missed my children terribly whom I had left in the care of their father in Conakry. I saw them everywhere: in the Métro, in the street and in the bars where I tried to keep warm by awkwardly smoking Gitanes cigarettes. At night, I was kept awake by nightmares. The same dream. I would get home, go over to my desk and start to tap on my typewriter. After a while I would be distracted by murmurs and stifled laughter. I would look up, and, in a corner of the room, would be my children who would then hurl themselves upon me and smother me with kisses.

Once or twice a month, the weekend brought me back Richard. Since he worked Saturday mornings, he could only catch the train from Charing Cross early afternoon. Given the length of the journey—train plus ferry plus train—he would arrive in Paris at nightfall. He hated the crazy atmosphere of the building and especially Waldomiro de Deus's, arrogant, almost impolite, expression. As a result, by the time he came to live with me, we were only too eager to move out. We found an elegant, tiny studio apartment on the rue de l'Université which belonged to a rich white Creole from Martinique, the Vicomte d'Origny. Every time he met Richard, he would complain of the strong smells from our kitchen which filled the staircase of his luxury town house. I was requested to tone down my sauces. 'The smell is stronger than the Dogon's,' he'd lament.

The Dogon was a Malian restaurant opposite the apartment. In the evening, there would be a procession of opulent-looking customers. I never set foot in it, not because of its exorbitant menu prices but because its lack of aromas and its bland atmosphere promised nothing good.

Richard was trilingual and soon found a job as a translator with an American company. I worked part-time at *Présence Africaine*, rue des Ecoles, selecting and publishing for the journal the articles sent in from all over Africa. I would like to say here how much I owe to M. and Mme Diop. Christiane Diop treated me like a young sister. She would cheer me up when the longing for my children became unbearable. She would mail parcels for them. At that time, the mail was far from secure in Africa but the words 'Présence Africaine' guaranteed safe passage. And I have never met a man as extraordinary as Alioune Diop. His intelligence was equalled only by his affability and his simplicity, he who was solicited by all the African heads of state. One evening, he came for dinner at the rue de l'Université and was delighted with the tuna casserole I had spent the whole day cooking in his honour.

As proof of how determined I was, I finished *The Hill of Massabielle*. I no longer have the French text of the play which, oddly enough, was staged years later by the Ubu Theatre Company, directed by Françoise Kourilsky, in New York. A dark tale of racism with a Guadeloupean mulatto as its hero. Gabriel was so delighted he cast two actors, a white man and a black man, to play the mulatto so as to underscore the symbol of the dual origin. The black man was played by a young actor, Sidiki Bakaba, who later went on to have a dazzling career. I was too busy to follow rehearsals nor to have a say in the direction, as Gabriel had wanted. *The Hill of Massabielle* was staged at the Hauts-de-Seine Theatre in Puteaux in the summer of 1971. In a theatre that could seat over seven hundred, a mere twenty were present, including some producers and an agent whom Gabriel had managed to get interested in his work. I wouldn't have remembered much about the show if a cruel and unexpected incident hadn't immortalized it. There were no cell phones then, no text messages. As a result, a relative of Mme Diop, who was attending with one of her daughters, had to come in person to tell her that her son David, hospitalized for several weeks for cancer of the pancreas, had just passed away. In light of this painful news, half the audience departed, leaving behind a mere handful of tearful spectators. I knew only too well that death was brutal, and, as the Bambara proverb says, it doesn't come drumming. Yet I still remember the shock I experienced that evening at the news.

To my great surprise, *The Hill of Massabielle* continued its career. A theatre lover by the name of James Campbell managed to obtain a contract for a festival at the American Cultural Center on the rue Dragon in Paris. As a result, there were two or three performances in a tiny theatre, packed this time. It was the start of a long friendship between James and I, since Richard, always a little suspicious, remained in the background. James was an unorthodox character. He wore suits fashioned oddly in a half-European, half-African style, and his weathered face and his hair bristling with short braids gave him a certain beauty. In the evenings, we would gather in a bar in the Latin Quarter located at equal distance between rue des Ecoles and *Présence Africaine*, rue de l'Université where Richard and I lived, and the Place Maubert where James lodged with his wife Hélène. We would discuss all kinds of topics, but mainly African politics.

'It'll be different with me. I'll take you to Africa,' James promised me, 'and I'll explain what's going on.'

Gifted with a deep voice, he was an excellent actor. During the 1966 festival in Dakar, he had performed in Césaire's *The Tragedy of King Christophe* opposite the famous Douta Seck; he had played in Conor Cruise O'Brien's *Murderous Angels* at the Palais de Chaillot. He was also a singer and a musician. It was not surprising that he was always surrounded by a fan club of adoring young girls, a fact that left Hélène perfectly indifferent. Above all, he was an excellent cook. His seasonings were a subtle blend of fresh mint, lemon and coriander, spices I seldom used at the time. On weekends, we worked up enough courage to combine our culinary inventions and cook endless feasts.

The Hill of Massabielle got me interested in the theatre. I liked the way the lines of dialogue and their concision worked. Consequently, I wrote *Dieu nous l'a donné* (God's Gift) for James which the editor Pierre-Jean Oswald published at the author's expense. James appeared as the main character, Mandela, an incestuous father, a sort of obeah man, a traditionalist, plotting the ruin of the young Europeanized doctor, seeking to seduce his daughter. The play had the good fortune to be accepted by a Martinican director, Yvon Labéjoff, who was to stage it during a festival in Martinique. To my great disappointment, James refused to play the character I had written for him and had to be replaced by another actor whose name I have forgotten. Fortunately, Toto Bissainthe was cast as the heroine whose talent as an actor and a singer go without saying.

This liking for the theatre may surprise the reader since I haven't written more than half a dozen plays. The reason is because I suddenly realized I was on the wrong track, and stopped. Although Gabriel was right in saying that the theatre implied an immediate and absolute communion between the playwright and his audience, it had to be uttered in a language that bonded both of them. On an island like Guadeloupe, the theatre should not make use of the language of the colonizer, even though for some it may have become commonplace. It should, rather, be expressed in Creole, the language forged by its people during the course of their tragic history.

When I recall those years, I am struck by how much of a workaholic I was. Except for my trips to the cinema (which remained my passion), I never stopped studying. I always had my nose stuck in a book, a magazine or a journal. It was as if I wanted to make up for all the time I had spent to accumulate experiences that would form the basis of my creativity. My priorities were writing my thesis and correcting *Heremakhonon.* And yet I found time to write another play, also published by Jean-Pierre Oswald and produced for the first time by a Senegalese company in Dakar: *Mort d'Oluwemi d'Ajumako.* Ajumako was the name of a small kingdom in Ghana. I had been inspired by an incident which had made headlines while I was living in Accra. After twenty years of reign, the sovereign of Ajumako had to ritually commit suicide and make room for his heir. Nana Prempeh III refused to comply with tradition.

He imprisoned his heir and had a wall built around his palace to protect him from the anger of his subjects. It was then that a mosquito flew into his bedroom, bit and poisoned him with the dengue hemorrhagic fever. He died suffocating in his own blood.

I also collaborated with Richard on the French translation of Eric William's masterly work, *Capitalism and Slavery: from Christopher Columbus to Fidel Castro*. I have no talent for translation. This art, which involves the fidelity and infidelity of the translator, requires finding the right word, attending to detail and knowing all the nuances of a language I do not possess. I learnt a lot. Although our names do not appear on the cover, I was infinitely proud of the final work when it was published by *Présence Africaine* in 1975.

During all this time, Richard and I took only one holiday. Araxie Drézian, an Armenian, who managed the bookstore at *Présence Africaine*, gave us the address of a studio apartment at Saint-Paul-de-Vence which friends of hers rented out. I knew the area of the Alpes-Maritimes, having spent a year at the sanatorium for students at Vence but had somewhat dark and gloomy memories of that stay and region. I was surprised, therefore, to discover its beautiful setting, its mild climate and its intense light. Rising lazily at noon, we would visit the Fondation Maeght and be dazzled by the artistic treasures it possessed. Instead of cooking meals, we gorged ourselves on fruit. Once or twice a week, we would take the bus down to Nice. Deterred by the cool water of the sea, I remained on the beach, admiring the blue immensity before me. Afterwards, we would lose our way among the crowd rambling up and down the Promenade des Anglais.

I was regaining my strength for the difficult times that lay ahead.

June 1976 finally arrived as a never-to-be-forgotten date. In front of Richard, James Campbell and Elikia M'Bokolo, a professor from Zaïre, I defended my thesis of comparative literature at the University of Paris III-Sorbonne. A few weeks earlier, my first novel had been published by Christian Bourgois in his 10/18 collection, thanks to Stanilas Adotevi, an intellectual from Benin and a frequent visitor to *Présence Africaine*. Stanislas Adotevi edited the series *La Voix des Autres* and was won over by my novel which he thought iconoclastic. Although my thesis was graded with distinction and received congratulations from the jury, my book was a total flop, despite the high hopes Stanislas had placed in it. I cannot recall reading a single review except one by an illustrious unknown writer in *Le Naïf*, a rag from Martinique, who showered me with insults and called me a whore and a voyeur. I was appalled. Was that literary criticism? The failure of a book has strange anaesthetic properties. The author, the victim, does not feel bad about it. On the contrary. A voice whispers to her that, since she is ahead of her time, she is misunderstood. Her ego is exaggerated. Consequently, she feels sorry for the writers who appear on TV and radio programmes to which she is not invited. She lives in total denial of reality. As for *Heremakhonon*, first rapidly discounted, then pulped by Bourgois, it attracted the attention of a handful of leftwing intellectuals, fascinated by its unusual portrayal of Africa.

As a result, and quite unexpectedly, I became friends with Robert Jaulin who directed the Department of Ethnology at the University of Paris VII. He often invited Richard and me for dinner to his vast apartment on the rue de Chanaleilles. My unsociability began to melt before the courtesy of those great minds who respected my opinion and listened to me in great earnestness. We would discuss African socialism, and Marxism which was starting to generate doubts in some but which for the majority represented the promise of the future.

'Tell us about NKrumah,' Dominique Desanti pleaded in her soft voice. 'He looks so intelligent.'

Robert came up with the idea of having his wife, Solange, and I teach a course on the oddly named ethno-cuisine. But neither of us was competent to teach a class at university level. Furthermore, what did ethno-cuisine mean? No one knew. Robert gave us a little speech, very academic, very technical, of which we understood very little. Nevertheless we took the plunge. Solange was to teach four hours every Monday morning and I four hours on Friday. We had no more than a dozen students; we met in the apartment of another ethnologist on the boulevard Saint-Michel. I can't remember what Solange was meant to teach but my reference was Guadeloupe where I hadn't set foot for nearly twenty years. Despite this absence, I had to explain how the offal of the hog—ears, snout, tail, trotters and tripe—with which it was convenient to feed the slaves, had become genuine delicacies. My job was to research the various culinary influences in Guadeloupe. Firs, African: callaloo, bébélé, congo soup, hog stew with breadfruit, pigeon peas, dove peas, peas and rice, to name the most popular, as well as other influences introduced by the East Indians who arrived later in the islands. I also had to describe the acclimation of certain exogenous species and the role they played in everyday cooking: breadfruit, coconut, cassava and tamarind. Above all I made a point of teaching the introduction and future monopoly of sugarcane imported from Cyprus. The job was arduous, and consisted of detaching every element from the landscape of Guadeloupe in order to examine it in greater detail.

I worked hard, consulting books by travellers and missionaries, genuine scriveners on the life and food of the slaves. The highlight of the class was, without question, the lunch on Fridays, intended to illustrate the previous lesson. Solange would join us, and, surrounded by the students, we would have a ball. The evening before, I sometimes cooked items at home that needed time and effort to prepare, such as salt pork, tripe and peas. I would carry it in plastic containers to class. I made an effort to keep to tradition: no cinnamon in the curried goat Colombo which Adélia used to reproach me for and no aged rum in anything. Those meals were a real pleasure. I recently received a letter from a former student, now almost seventy, vividly recalling those days.

On the last day of class, Solange and I combined menus. The tapenade of pureed olives rubbed shoulders with the cod fritters, the aioli with pork stew. The rum and the pastis flowed freely. Afterwards, slightly tipsy, we made our way with the students to the Luxembourg Gardens, to take photos next to the circular basin. Troubled by our overexcited group, the children held on cautiously to their boats. Unfortunately, the ethno-cuisine classes lasted only a trimester and did not resume the following year. Solange was too tired for she was expecting her second child. As a replacement, Robert asked me to speak on African socialism. That was much less fun.

Living on such close terms with Guadeloupe only heightened my desire to return. I have already said that I hadn't set foot on the island for almost twenty years. I hadn't gone out of fear of being hurt. My parents were dead. Their town house in Pointe-à-Pitre had been sold and their change-of-air house in Sarcelles, where my father would clothe in a khaki drill suit and a pith helmet to play the gentleman farmer, no longer existed. All that was left was a majestic family vault. I hadn't the strength to go and kneel in front of it. So I had to summon a great deal of courage to sit beside Richard on an Air France flight crowded with native islanders and tourists. At the time, Guadeloupe ranked high on the list of Club Med attractions. The endless strikes in the tourist sector and the acts of violence by the unemployed had not yet tarnished its reputation.

I remember we arrived at the airport in Le Raizet late afternoon. The sky was bleeding red into the sea. My heart was pounding with emotion. That first evening, however, I was spared the agonizing confrontation with my memories. My brother, who was to be our host, had settled down in Basse-Terre at the other end of the island, far from the family birthplace, much to my parents' disapproval. He was the black sheep of the family and my parents always found fault with his behaviour. They preferred their older children: Auguste, the first Guadeloupean to pass the *aggregation* competitive exam; Jean, who perished in the death camps during the Second World War; and Sandrino, a promising writer. They blamed my brother René for marrying a diaphanous mulatto woman who stood out like a sore thumb in our jet-black midst. (She belonged to a clan of penniless local dignitaries on the leeward side of the island, had a handle to her name and one of her brothers was a discalced monk.)

As we ascended towards the volcano, La Soufrière, dusk was falling. By the time we reached our destination, it was pitch black. The house must have been close to the sea since we could hear its loud voice, mourning. The next day we were woken by a terrific din: my sister-in-law and two young servants were cleaning and washing everything that could be cleaned and washed, banging buckets and basins, revving the vacuum cleaner and sweeping and scraping. She was surprised at our haggard looks and she was not wrong to be so. The sun, whose fierceness I had forgotten, was flooding our surroundings. The street was a dazzling white. Down below, the sea was a gleaming sheet of corrugated iron. Soon the heat was unbearable. My brother and his wife had six children; together with half a dozen adopted children, their relatives as well as godchildren and family, the house was packed. Twice a day, in order to feed all these mouths, my sister-in-law would order Margarita pizzas from the Gargantua close by. I was shocked. I had in mind my ethno-cuisine classes, and I offered to help her.

'You know how to cook?' she asked suspiciously.

From that day on, four of us were busy in the small shack-kitchen at the back of the yard. I was soon very upset, however, because nobody seemed to like my compositions. Day after day they were scraped almost intact into the garbage bin. One ten-year-old Simon even dared to complain openly: 'Why aren't we eating Margarita pizzas any more? At least, *they* were good.'

Appalled, I plucked up courage to complain to my sister-in-law. She looked at me straight in the eyes, perhaps for the first time, and then decreed a list of taboos: Never mix sweet and savoury. Never mix meat and fish; nor meat and shellfish. Plantains and mangoes are never to be eaten green. Tuna fish in a curry is unthinkable. Never use tomatoes in a fish court-bouillon, only annatto butter. Coq au vin is cooked in wine and not aged rum. While I almost collapsed in tears, she continued in her shrill voice: since Richard and I were not married and lived in sin, we were not behaving appropriately. On Sundays we did not attend high mass nor holy rosary on weekday evenings. We wore sloppy clothes, faded T-shirts, ugly shorts and, I in particular, inelegant clogs.

After such a conversation, any further cohabitation was out of the question.

Nobody kept us from leaving.

Two days later, Richard and I piled our baggage onto a bus that rattled its way along the winding 60 kilometres to Pointe-à-Pitre. I was in low spirits. For me, it seemed a highway to hell. Despite the ominous threat of an eruption by the volcano that had remained dormant for years—there was talk of evacuating the whole region—Basse-Terre seemed to shelter me from nostalgia and bitter memories. This small town, on the edge of a majestic sea, preserved the anonymity of the provinces. By 8 p.m., its streets were deserted, every door and window closed. In Pointe-à-Pitre, I would have been grabbed by the ghosts of the past. I still hadn't found the strength to make my way to the cemetery, and this weak-mindedness tortured me. On the other hand, I went on a pilgrimage to the neighbourhood where my parents used to live, once so clean and prosperous. It appeared to be partly abandoned. The house where

I was born belonged to a dentist and needed a new coat of paint. My eyes brimming with tears, I looked up at the balcony wrapped around the second floor previously potted with bougainvillea, from where I used to gaze at the crowds in the street that my strict education forbade me from joining. During carnival season, the *moko zombies* perched on their stilts drew level with our balustrade and held out their calloused palms for small coins. But I was scared of them and their huge black wigs tied low with striped scarves, and I would run to hide inside.

'Don't be silly,' my mother would say. 'What on earth do you think they'll do? They're having fun, that's all, and asking for money.'

I also went on a pilgrimage to Sarcelles. Since the Conseil Général had approved to re-route the road to Basse-Terre, a large macadamized highway ran through the middle of my parents' former property. The gracious wooden house with its dormer windows and circular balcony I ran along as a child had been torn down. A field tangled with hog plums and guava trees had replaced the perfectly kept garden where I played hide and seek. Only a lofty flame tree had been spared.

In Pointe-à-Pitre, we were guests of José whom I had known in Paris when I was writing my thesis. While I sat alone on the terrace of the Café Mahieu, he had asked permission to join me. Sure, he was quite handsome, tall and well built, but I very quickly made it clear that, if he was trying to seduce me, he was wasting his time. I was no longer interested in love affairs. I remained true to one man. He made no objection, and we became the best of friends. He dragged me to the meetings of the General Association of Guadeloupean Students. Thanks to him, I realized that Guadeloupe and Martinique were not meant to remain the eternal confetti of empire as I always believed they were, and that they were entitled to demand a different status. Together, we became members of an independence movement: the Popular Union for the Liberation of Guadeloupe (UPLG) and I have often been blamed for it. I must confess that I was not entirely driven by political convictions. There was also the desire to be integrated in a group of individuals with similar ideas and actions, I who so often had the feeling of not belonging.

José was married to Catherine, a pretty, sophisticated girl from Martinique with mascara-lengthened eyelashes and scarlet nail polish. He was now a member of the UPLG's management committee. Oddly enough, we never spoke about the experiences I had recently lived through. For him, Africa boiled down to Algeria where the 'refuseniks', the Antilleans who had refused to enrol in military service, had combined forces with the Algerian FLN. His house was packed with party members and sympathizers, 'Patriots', recognizable by their *bitako* rustic look: the women had picky hair, left uncombed, and wore no lipstick, while the men were dressed in ungainly suits of khaki drill at a time when tapered jeans were in vogue. During the lunch break, they would surge into the dining room and order the ever-popular Margarita pizzas from a restaurant opposite.

The cohabitation between José and me soon hit a sour note. He called me a 'holiday maker', a term which to my ears sounded like 'foreigner'. Whereas I had always been open about my family upbringing, he lost patience with me because I spoke French–French and not Creole; he became annoyed when I nodded off and yawned during the never-ending *lewoz* dances to which he would drag me, evening after evening, along with all his friends. He was barely polite with Richard, and I sensed it was hard for him to imagine me marrying a white man. In his eyes, Richard belonged to the race of exploiters and was responsible for all the crimes, past and present, of colonialism.

In order to dispel the gathering storm between us, I decided to cook a meal, a sort of banquet that would reunite us as well as the Patriots. It turned out to be a bad idea. Nobody liked the conch mixed with haddock with chives and small onions. Omélie, the servant, cleared away the plates virtually untouched.

'It's a bit unusual,' Catherine murmured, embarrassed.

'It's called "nouvelle cuisine",' José commented, offhandedly.

Afterwards, the guests went out onto the balcony to down bottles of rum. It was then that a wave of questions about *Heremakhonon* rolled towards me. I was amazed. I thought nobody had read it.

'In *Heremakhonon* Veronica is a negative heroine, isn't she? That's not right.'

'Why did you put so much sex in your novel?'

'After Saliou's death, why didn't the people revolt?'

'What's the meaning of the Malian street cleaner? His presence in the book doesn't make sense!'

And on and on.

I put up as brave a front as I could. 'Like a lion,' Richard assured me later in amusement. I was not interested in portraying positive heroines. I had depicted a woman such as I knew, with her lot of pessimism and optimism. Sex? It was strange that, in this Guadeloupean society, I was being blamed for giving sex more than its due. In everyday life, it played such a major role. The men were virtually sex maniacs and the women too often victims. *Heremakhonon* was a novel about a failed revolution; that was obvious, I thought. As for the Malian street-cleaner, he was a metaphor for the watertight partition between the classes. Veronica and he lived parallel lives, each locked in their obsessions and problems. After those questions, I felt I had been attacked and couldn't sleep a wink, determined to escape as soon as possible. But where could I go? Why not to Marie-Galante? My friend, the poet Guy Tirolien, had not yet been debilitated by his illness and taken refuge on his island. So I couldn't go and visit him. But the little island I had once known had left me with dazzling memories. When I was a child, the crossing was by steamship and lasted for hours. Passengers sat wherever there was room, between crates of cackling chickens and high-pitched squealing hogs. Those who were seasick would lean over the railings and their great jets of vomit were frayed by the wind. That time was well and truly over. Ultramodern catamarans now had rows of red plastic benches. Three television screens broadcast videos and the crew, in dashing blue and white uniforms, handed round paper bags for those who felt seasick.

I set off for La Treille, the neighbourhood where my mother and grandmother were born, and was struck by its extreme poverty. I had known my mother as an accomplished middle-class teacher, looking down in contempt on those who had not been as successful as her. Seeing the humble thatched shacks, similar to the one where she had probably been born, I almost forgave her arrogance. How far she had come! What a strong will she must have had! It was there that I had the idea of writing a book about her and her mother. It took me years to complete and resulted in *Victoire, My Mother's Mother*, published in 2006.

I had no trouble finding Michelle again. As wide as she was tall, her waist now three times larger than the late Adélia's. She was married to a carpenter by the name of Paco and was mother to a string of children. We flew into each other's arms. 'Maman suffered a great deal before she died,' she cried. 'She didn't deserve it, she was such a good soul. There aren't many mothers like her.'

Oblivion cleans up memories, it's a well-known fact. Michelle no longer recalled how Adélia used to scold her and how cruel and unsympathetic she had been.

She had transformed Adélia's former restaurant, The Hungry Clam, into a pizzeria and served up the inevitable Margarita pizzas for lunch. Since I wasn't at all pleased, she explained: 'That's what people like nowadays. Things have changed a great deal. The women go off to work and haven't time to spend in the kitchen. They don't earn enough to pay for a servant. There's nobody to cook. Pizzas are quick and easy to eat. Whenever they want Guadeloupean cuisine, they go to the local supermarket and buy black pudding, shredded saltfish in a can and frozen batter for making cod fritters and dumplings. And what about you who used to love cooking, do you still like it?'

I blurted out as if at confession: 'Still the same.'

That's how I organized a dinner at Michelle's. She invited her husband's six brothers and their wives. The latter turned up wearing very attractive long shapeless white *golle* dresses and black-and-white-check madras head ties. In order not to scare these palates unaccustomed to culinary eccentricities, I toned down my passion to invent. The appetizer therefore consisted of local black pudding garnished with a cucumber salad flavoured with hot peppers and lemon. Then followed a breadfruit soufflé and a tuna stew in which I couldn't help slipping in some tiny Chinese eggplants. In spite of these small caprices, the guests devoured my dishes and asked for more. After the meal, the women hoisted their dresses above their knees and began to dance. Two of Paco's brothers picked up the *ka* drum and began to beat in rhythm. Never had I been so charmed by the *gwo ka* in the glow of the night.

There was no hotel in Marie-Galante, so we spent the end of the holiday at Michelle's place in sweltering promiscuity. Children were crying and sleeping everywhere. The shadows of the night were softened by blue and green night lights. Michelle, like my brother's wife, was up at four in the morning, making coffee which she sipped outdoors. I went and joined her under the almond tree and we talked about our lives. She was very proud of Gertulien, her eldest son, an excellent student who had received a scholarship to study German in Mainz from where he dispatched enthusiastic missal after enthusiastic missal. I imagined that teenager, born and raised in Marie-Galante, catapulted into a foreign city and liking it. Sometimes Paco would come and join us and share entertaining stories. I planned to include them in a book for young readers, entitled *Tales from the Carpenter's Plane*, but I never did. I seldom give up on a project I have devised, even if it takes a very long time. This particular case, however, put me in a predicament. Should I translate and transpose into French those stories that were told in a sparkling Creole? They would surely lose their flavour. Should they be copied out as such? If so, the readership would be seriously reduced. Michelle and Paco, who hadn't a clue about 'literary ambition', were of little help. In the end, I wrote nothing. *Tales from the Carpenter's Plane* was never published and remains one of my great regrets.

That stay, despite its conviviality and warmth, signalled a farewell: a farewell to childhood dreams, to the myth of a timeless Guadeloupe, good enough for reassuring intellectuals and ethnologists. The island was constantly changing. I had to keep in touch with the changes, understand them and antic-ipate the consequences. In a word, the mysterious importance of the Margarita pizzas had to be solved.

I returned to settle in Guadeloupe a few years later, following the publication of *Segu* in 1984. I bought an old change-of-air house in Montebello, in the region of Petit Bourg where I had spent my hol-idays as a child. The area around Petit Bourg has a subtle, somewhat old-fashioned charm which speaks directly to my heart. In Montebello, I often invited my close circle of friends for a meal, among whom was Michel Rovelas who loved my cooking and referred to it with poetic license.

I had learnt my lesson. Just as my cooking was not genuine Guadeloupean, I too would never be a genuine Guadeloupean. But what does the word 'genuine' mean? Nobody has been able to explain it to me. In this age, where everything is interconnected and exchanged, is it possible or even desirable?

The Triumph of the Sweet and Savoury

Since the political situation in Guinea had seriously deteriorated, Condé, my first husband, had to flee and take refuge in the Ivory Coast. It was from there that the children, one after another, came to join me in Paris. Denis first, landing at the airport dressed in a pale-green boubou of bazin fabric in the depth of winter's cold. Then the three girls, shortly afterwards. They brought me great happiness but also the prospect of a heavy financial responsibility. Richard earned a good living as translator with Kodak-Pathé. But what was enough for a couple was not good enough to feed so many mouths. We had to abandon our studio on the rue de l'Université which we both liked so much and move to a vast but nondescript rental in Puteaux. In order to confront my new role as a suburban mother of a large family, I could no longer be content with working part-time at *Présence Africaine* nor teaching classes for practically nothing as I had done with Robert and was now doing for Claude Abastado at Nanterre and Jeanne-Lydie Goré at Paris III-Sorbonne, intellectuals who had taken an interest in my career. I needed a permanent job with a regular salary. It is difficult to imagine that in those providential times there was virtually no unemployment. I had no trouble finding a job with a new African magazine. It was neither left-wing nor militant, centre-left at the most. I never knew exactly where its funds came from. Its director was a native of the Comoro Islands, a bit of a crook, quite handsome, his hair parted to one side, and very knowledgeable about the situation in what was then called the Third World.

I was somewhat disappointed because he put me in charge of the literary column instead of the political page. From early morning, the luxurious offices of the magazine were invaded by a crowd of visitors, supplicants and commentators of recent political events in Africa. I discovered that Guinea was not the only dictatorship. Paris harboured a bunch of opponents to the current regimes, as well as those sentenced to voluntary exile who had fled to safeguard their freedom and even their lives. The peremptory nature of their comments and their categorical and cursory analyses made me laugh since they appeared to be totally divorced from their countries with no power whatsoever over their fates. I was far from imagining that several of them would become presidents of the republics they were criticizing. At noon, we crowded into the restaurants and lunched briefly on andouillette sausages and French fries.

I liked my job of reviewing books I thought important, writing author's portraits and doing interviews wherever possible. That was how I met

Mariama Ba. She had just published her book *So Long a Letter* (an African bestseller), and checked into a hotel in the Latin Quarter for its promotion. We had breakfast in a cafe. All around us the boulevard Saint-Michel was a hive of activity: students running to the Sorbonne, professors walking serenely, their briefcases under their arms. I envied this academic frenzy, since my student years had not been the best of times.

A mutual sympathy drew Mariama Ba and me closer. As writers we were very different yet we shared the same fear of others and suffered from the same feeling of insecurity.

'If they hadn't forced me,' she said, 'I would never have had the courage to publish my book. It would have stayed in a drawer.'

'That would have been a pity!' I exclaimed, because I loved her book.

At the magazine, I did everything I could to win over my editor-in-chef who was very reluctant. 'It's an old woman's story,' he said, shrugging. 'What would people say if we made such a fuss about it?'

An old woman's story! He hadn't understood a thing. He hadn't appreciated this early cry for the liberation of African women and the elimination of traditions that were stifling them. Mariama Ba and I promised to meet again after she had finished her tour around Europe.

'Come and see me in Senegal,' she pleaded. 'We have so much in common.'

I was stupefied when the news came of her death a few months later. In the years to follow, in homage to this modest and astute woman, *So Long a Letter* has always been on my course list.

Unknowingly, I began to acquire a reputation for virulence for I had the audacity to write what I thought about the novels and essays I was in charge of reading. My editor-in-chief did not appreciate this frankness. 'Water down your wine,' he advised me. 'Turn your pen seven times in your inkwell. People will end up thinking you're jealous and frustrated.'

After *Heremakhonon* I wrote *A Season in Rihata*, published by Robert Laffont where a fellow Antillean was the director of a collection. Since this second novel proved to be no more successful than the first, people might have thought that I was taking my revenge wherever I could.

My compulsive desire to work, however, did not die down. I dashed from one end of Paris to the other, jumping onto buses and scrambling down the steps of the Métro despite the heavy Nagra tape recorder hanging from one shoulder. Twice I went to Belgium and once to Sweden, which left me with unpleasant memories since the conference on feminine literature to which I was invited turned out to be a nest of militant lesbians who treated me with the utmost contempt. Nevertheless, I had never experienced such a feeling of freedom. I was not entirely reconciled with Paris. Too-bitter memories floated around certain districts. But the city no longer scared me. Deep down, I was convinced I would continue my life elsewhere. My existence would be turned drastically upside down. I would go and live in another country and do things besides hatching cultural articles for a second-rate magazine. I would discover the world and maintain original and enriching relationships.

In early spring I met Zineb. She was the wife of a high-ranking dignitary from Tunisia, governor of the southern province of Gabès. She had written an essay describing the condition of women in Tunisia, her native land. She was full of praise for President Bourguiba, who was the first to have dared to change their status and make them full-fledged citizens. I read her essay in one go and it left me with a deep impression. At the time, I knew nothing about the Arabs. Although in Guadeloupe there was a large community of Lebanese called Syrians, resulting from some unknown historical mistake, society was so partitioned that I never hung out with any of them at school. In Pointe-à-Pitre, José's apartment, located in the heart of the old town, was above the shop of one of these Lebanese, a dark poky little place cluttered with all sorts of bolts of gaudy coloured fabric, oriental slippers, ottomans, rugs and an assortment of useless knick-knacks. We used to see the owner smoking a narghile at the back of the store while his wife, winsome and voluminous, lorded it over the cash register. They had countless children who swore in Creole and fought on the pavement. José hated the Syrian Lebanese. He described to me angrily how they had arrived as hawkers with their goods tied in a bundle. Today they were considered to be some of the worst exploiters on the island.

'Worst exploiters?' I protested in jest. 'You're exaggerating!'

'Not at all. They employ a lot of domestic employees and sales people who are paid peanuts.'

Zineb made a reservation for us at the restaurant in the Crillon Hotel where she was staying. She was beautiful, sophisticated and elegant, from her hennaed hair to her leather ankle boots. My meeting with her was one of those unforgettable moments, one among many that made a mark on my life. Not because of the immediate affection I felt for her, not because of this initial and exciting journey deep into the world of North African women she introduced me to, but because for the first time I ate lamb stew or navarin. We both ordered it without much thought, since it was the daily special. Then we both found it so delicious that Zineb made a request to the waiter to fetch the chef. He emerged from the downstairs kitchen, wearing his chef's hat, shaking hands left and right like a star as he made his way over to our table. Then he solemnly declaimed: 'Lamb stew is a simple, savoury dish after the monotonous heaviness of winter dishes. The vegetable ingredients are selected young so as to match the tender, delicate meat of the lamb.'

Zineb pretended to take down notes. I dared to ask a question, true to my habit of adding a personal touch everywhere: 'Can you add diced smoked bacon?'

'Never!' the chef jumped in horror. 'It would totally change the taste.'

Then he asked us what country we were from. He was probably intrigued that a black woman and an Arab could be so fond of a jewel of traditional French gastronomy. At that moment I established a principle from which I have never wavered: whatever one's origin, one always has the right to appropriate a dish. Either you reproduce it faithfully or you add variations of your own invention. Dishes have no nationality; they are not designed for a specific group nor are they served up for the taste and whim of any one in particular. Lamb navarin is now one of my favourite dishes. I often cook it for my American friends. When I do so, I keep scrupulously to the original recipe for I know how much they admire France and I wouldn't risk betraying it.

During the following two days, Zineb and I stuck together. I accompanied her to the department stores where she spent a fortune on fashionable trinkets. I took her to the *Présence Africaine* bookstore where we bought everything we could, Zineb buying my beloved African authors, and I, books by Arab writers I had never heard of. We waved goodbye in tears at Orly airport, vowing to meet again as soon as possible.

A few weeks later the magazine sent me back to Tunisia to cover the festival in Hammamet. I arrived late afternoon at the cultural centre, which then was merely a modest fishing village. The festival took place in a magnificent location where the terraced seats looked out over the sea. An official took me to the villa I had been allocated. I was surprised by its luxury. I learnt later that it had been designed for Senegalese president Léopold Sédar Senghor who had honoured it with his presence during the previous festival. I never discovered the mystery of why it had been allocated to me. It consisted of a string of large rooms open to the breeze and the serene, sweet-smelling sea down below. One of them was hollowed out into a kind of pool whose water had been scented. I slipped in with a feeling of well-being seldom experienced.

Then I rambled around the village. It seemed I could reach out and touch the night sky studded with gold. It was almost as hot as in Guadeloupe, but a heat that softly seeped and spread over you like an intimate piece of lingerie. The bars were lit *a giorno*. The terraces were crowded with men smoking narghiles or playing cards and dice. In the street, young men swaggered astride their Vespas and Lambrettas. Children were screaming and running in and out.

I entered a bar and ordered a mint tea.

'Are you from Djerba?' the waiter asked me familiarly.

Why Djerba? I thought. At the time I was not aware that the south of Tunisia, like all the southern regions of the Maghreb, was inhabited by people of colour, visibly of African origin. That evening I didn't mind being mistaken for a native daughter. I noted there were very few women among the customers. Those who were present were accompanied by a man and emptied their glasses like well-behaved children. I slowly made my way back, breathing in deeply the scent of honeysuckle and jasmine that was such a change from the smell of tar in the streets of Paris.

The next day a message came from Zineb: she couldn't come to Hammamet. It was a national holiday in Gabès and there was no way she could avoid her obligations. But she invited me to come and spend the weekend with her. She would send a limousine to fetch me. This was the second disappointment, the first that Richard had stayed behind in Paris. Was it because of my mood at the time that I remember nothing of the festival, except its spectacular setting? What did I attend? Plays, concerts, ballets? Was it solely for artistic companies from the African continent? Or was it open to all? I couldn't say. All I recall is the vast expanse of sea changing its Donkeyskin gowns to match the colour of the sky, and the scent of jasmine that floated in the air.

When the festival was over, a magnificent limousine driven by a chauffeur in soldier's uniform came to fetch me. He apologized politely in advance: the drive would be long and arduous because of the heat. Gabès was situated at the edge of the desert. We stopped in Nabeul to pick up Mansour, one of Zineb's young brothers, who immediately launched into a virulent attack on the regime: 'We students have just begun a strike. This government is nothing but a dictatorship,' he declared, settling his buttocks on the car's fawn-coloured cushions. 'Zineb of course won't tell you that since she is married to a relative of the president. But it's the truth.'

I fell asleep while he listed the president's crimes. When I woke up, he too had fallen asleep, mouth wide open like a child. We drove the last few kilometres in silence. All around us the landscape had become desert-like. Here and there leafless trees emerged from the stony ground. Like fleeting ghosts, animals that I had trouble identifying, probably goats, capered about in the dazzling glare of the sun.

We arrived in Gabès for lunch and it was strange to see buildings suddenly appear and life resume after hours of oppressive solitude. In the narrow streets, boys were running after one another, little old ladies were trotting along and a donkey driver was whipping his stubborn animal who was refusing to budge. Zineb and her husband were waiting for us on the balcony of their magnificent villa, situated in a genuine oasis of flowers and greenery. With his light brown skin and his black hair smoothed back into a bow, Ali, Zineb's husband, had the manners and appearance of an oriental prince. After the shabby

Islam of Guinea, I discovered a majestic Islam which fascinated me. Zineb's husband turned to Mansour: 'I bet,' he said smiling, 'he bored you stiff with his political speeches. If he wants to see a dictatorship, he should go to Morocco or Algeria.'

I was unsure how to reply. But I was shocked. I had always thought of Algeria as an example, a country that had won its independence after a terrible war of liberation. Its leaders could not have become dictators.

Waiters dressed in cream-coloured gandurahs served us refreshments of cheese, fruit and salad. The sugary taste of one of them intrigued me but I didn't have time to ask questions as we were swept into a car and driven off to attend a series of events. Zineb was president of an orphanage, a hostel for disabled teenagers, a retirement home and a school for girls. As soon as she set foot outside the car, she was mobbed by press photographers. At every stop she gave a speech, always the same one, speaking highly of the regime's clear-sightedness and benevolence. She pointed me out to the spectators as a writer and journalist friend who had come to take part in the festivities. Each time I had to stand up, wave and smile, something I do really badly. I had the feeling I was playing a role I was not prepared for. I had to explain to an inquisitive onlooker where Guadeloupe was— he had never heard of it. Zineb lingered for a long time at the Habib-Bourguiba school of which she was especially proud. It numbered around forty students in two classes. Besides reading grammar and history, they learnt French. Consequently, the students sang the president's praises in two languages.

'No cooking class?' I asked in amazement.

'No,' Zineb responded sharply. 'I want to squash the too-common argument that women should be in the kitchen. In our countries, women seem good for only two things: reproducing and cooking. I wanted to prove that we can train girls to fill any type of job.'

Such an argument seemed specious to me. Why can't a doctor in philosophy or a Nobel Prize winner in chemistry treat their guests to a delicious meal? But I didn't want to quarrel with Zineb whom I was so pleased to see again.

We walked towards the car. Night had fallen and a surprising freshness came up from the ground. Zineb took me by the hand. 'I know what you're thinking, but tonight I haven't invited anyone. There will just be us four and my two eldest children, Mohammed and Armelle, whom you haven't met yet.'

The dinner had the charm of an evening out of the *Arabian Nights*. The room was lit by the soft light of lanterns. We were sunk deep in ample sofas and the servants set the dishes on low tables in front of us. Zineb filled my plate. 'Here, try this,' she said. 'I had it made especially for you.'

I took a mouthful and jumped.

'What is it? What's the name of the dish?'

'It's a tajine,' she explained. 'A tajine of dried apricots and almonds. Like Morocco, we have a very special culinary tradition and some people go so far as to say we have borrowed it from them. It's a delicate blend of flavours, a mixture of sweet and savoury.'

I had often introduced dried fruit in my culinary compositions. When it was a question of fish especially, I got the impression of breaking a taboo, of offending, of committing a fault. That evening I learnt that other people were doing the same.

'In tajines, the fruit is treated like a vegetable,' she continued. 'You add honey or sugar to the meat or fish sauce at a very precise moment. You shouldn't confuse the sweet and savoury with the sweet and sour found in China and India, for instance.'

I helped myself again, exhilarated by the rich taste which melted in my mouth.

'This tradition dates back to when?' I asked.

'Probably to the Middle Ages. Perhaps a little later. In the regions to the south, you can find the remains of aqueducts which irrigated the sugarcane plantations. They probably date back to the seventeenth century. There are all sorts of tajines: with dates, with hearts of artichokes, peas, prunes, sesame seeds and sardines, which my grandmother was so fond of. But the one I like best is the tajine with dried apricots and almonds.'

The next day I flew back to Paris. Despite the weight of my luggage loaded down with two tajine cooking pots given to me by Zineb, I felt light-hearted and overjoyed. I had the impression I had discovered a treasure trove. What might have seemed a personal eccentricity was closely akin to the taste of other human beings. In a certain way, I had invented the tajine. I could make endless variations of it and combine the meat and fish of my choosing. A world rich in possibilities had opened up.

A few weeks later for Richard's birthday I invited some friends for dinner. I had wanted to invite my sister Gillette who was in Paris for an important meeting with the families of victims of Sékou Touré, one of whom was Diallo Telli. But she had someone call to tell me she had another engagement. Our relations hadn't improved. In *Heremakhonon*, she thought she recognized her portrait as well as my sister Ena's and held it against me. She disliked Richard whom she mockingly called 'The Prince Consort' and decided my children did not show her enough respect. I didn't care. I had cooked a tajine of my own invention with artichoke hearts and dried apricots. The somewhat surprising combination was delicious. My guests tucked in with delight.

DAL IS DAL

In order to celebrate our first wedding anniversary, Richard and I decided to give ourselves a magical journey that would fill our heads with unforgettable memories. We also wanted to make up for the morose atmosphere of our honeymoon, if that is what you can call the few days we spent at Lyons-la-Forêt in a house loaned by a friend. Although we were in the middle of August, the weather was overcast and rainy. The beech trees of Lyons-la-Forêt, usually so beautiful, mounted an austere, heavy guard around the property. Richard's parents, Marjorie and Cyril, who appeared to show no objection to their only son marrying a black woman, older than him and mother of four, drank to our health with our witnesses Claude and Ingrid Wauthier and Elikia and Bernadette M'Bokolo, the only wedding guests. Unfortunately, they didn't speak a word of French, so the conversation was somewhat limited. Since Denis was somewhere in Africa and Leila at Basse-Terre in Guadeloupe, only Sylvie and Aïcha remained. They appeared to be in a sullen mood. They probably thought they were losing their mother. The two Arab cooks from Beuzeville had difficulty getting the barbecue to grill since the wood was of poor quality and had trouble burning.

Around three in the afternoon, a car drew up at the front gate. On board, in the arms of her Senegalese father with his usual swagger was my one-year-old granddaughter, Raky. Leila had given birth to a baby girl. Needless to say, the unexpected arrival of this baby, however adorable, to spend the remainder of the week with us, didn't help matters. Richard and I must be the only newlyweds who spent their honeymoon with one of their grandchildren. Raky was a capricious, headstrong baby. I have some comical photos of her trying to climb over the cross of an American soldier's grave in one of the region's many war cemeteries

For me, however, this second marriage implied a genuine renaissance. I emerged again from my mother's womb, no longer scared of landing in the claws of a wicked midwife but serenely prepared for the future. I was about to renounce the two maledictive names of Boucolon and Condé for a perfectly neutral English patronymic surname: Philcox. The disillusions and disappointments I had experienced were peeling away from my body. I piled them into a heap and set light to them like a bunch of dead leaves.

By common agreement, we decided to visit India. The choice was not surprising. Richard had a deep fascination for India, like a man for a beautiful, mysterious mistress he had been unable to seduce. I remembered the dazzling images of the Youth Festival in Warsaw when the Indians had paraded in their traditional costumes. India had always been present for me. My parents had adopted the three children of Mawoude, our Indian caretaker ('coolie' was the common name at the time), at their change-of-air house in Sarcelles after their mother died. They had entrusted the two boys, Jacques and Carmélien, to vocational schools and taken in the daughter, Danielle, barely four, as part of the family without troubling to adopt her legally as is often the case in Guadeloupe. As a result, Danielle had grown up with me, like a younger sister, despite her origins. Thanks to her I often visited her uncles, aunts and cousins, the numerous Guadeloupeans of Indian origin in Petit-Bourg. We used to eat a dish called trempage even though my mother found it disgusting, a combination of saltfish, plantains and tomatoes, served on shiny banana leaves and then eaten by hand. I also deeply admired Mahatma Gandhi and his doctrine of nonviolence, as well as Pandit Nehru whose biography had enthralled me. In short, I endowed India with a humanity that I looked forward to rubbing shoulders with.

A few days before we left, we went for dinner at our friend Raj's, an Indian who worked for Unesco, to tell him the news of our departure. He is a skilled cook and he treated us to a tamarind-flavoured lamb which has driven me to despair. Despite all my efforts, I have been incapable of imitating it.

To our surprise, at the announcement of our departure he cautioned us: 'India is a complicated country. The best rubs shoulders with the worst. Most of all don't imagine it to be a Mecca of Marvels.'

'What do you mean?'

He refused to look us straight in the eye. 'Go and you will understand.'

Falling out of love is the same as falling in love. There is no prior announcement, no explanation, simply an imprisonment of the heart in a stifling embrace. I cannot say exactly when the long-awaited voyage became painfully heavy-going. Perhaps it was due to the flight: our plane was delayed and we had to spend the night on the uncomfortable green benches at Cairo airport. It finally landed in the dirty grey light of dawn. The immigration officials kept us for over an hour. When we finally emerged from the airport, Mumbai appeared filthy. Trails of garbage and piles of cow pats soiled the streets. Despite the early hour, it was very hot. The electric blue of the sky scorched the eyes. Entire families were shamelessly soaping themselves at the public fountains. Men were zigzagging on bicycle rickshaws. Bearded ascetics kneeling in the dust, oblivious to the dirt and chaos, were praying, their eyes half-closed.

We had booked a room at the Taj , the very same which years later was the target of a terrorist attack. The usual cosmopolitan crowd filled the dining room. An English group politely invited us to sit at their table. Their manners betrayed the arrogance of the wealthy but with a smile. Great connoisseurs of India, they were frequent visitors and clearly more enthusiastic than our friend Raj.

'It's an extraordinary country,' they assured us. 'You'll see, once you've experienced it, there's no getting away from it.'

Despite our fatigue, we decided to visit the city. As soon as we left the hotel, a throng of street peddlers swooped down on us, offering all sorts of food which, normally, would have drawn my attention. But I was disconcerted by the looks of the passers-by. It was not the usual curiosity towards a mixed couple. We were used to that. A mixed couple can never go unnoticed. It can never melt into the crowd anonymously. It is always and everywhere an object of oddness. These looks were very different—they marked me out. Sparing Richard, they fastened onto me. These looks were filled with facets I was unable to elucidate, as if I was an object of stupor and amusement. A group of boys in white-striped, apple-green uniforms burst out laughing at me and then ran off.

The worst was soon to come. We arrived at a crowded crossroads. Tired from the journey and probably because of the unbearable heat, Richard slipped and collapsed onto the pavement. Nobody stopped, no one paid attention to this man, this stranger, lying on the ground, perhaps seriously ill. The pedestrians merely walked round him so as not to step on him. In a panic I ran to a public faucet, soaked my handkerchief and managed to revive him after a few minutes. We stumbled back to the hotel amid the sound of car horns, the ringing of bicycle rickshaws and the clamour of the crowd.

At dinner, none of the English sympathized with us when we described our misadventure. One of them, calmly peeling a pear, said: 'There is so much misery in this country. People are born and die just about anywhere. Perhaps it is outrageous but the Indians are hardened to suffering. It's not surprising that nobody rushed to help you. We're not in London where people sympathize with the slightest incident involving a dog or a cat.'

We had carefully prepared for our trip and bought a railway pass in Paris which would allow us to visit all of northern India from Mumbai to Calcutta by way of Udaipur, Jaipur, New Delhi, Agra and Varanasi. Early next morning, we caught the train from the main station. Street peddlers everywhere. Others offering a mixture of tea and condensed milk or 'chai'. In our train compartment, a large family was eating out of a mess of greasy paper and cardboard plates, the smell of which made me feel sick. They stopped eating to stare at me. I was really starting to find the way people stared at me quite unbearable. Once again I can only say they hesitated between hilarity and repulsion. As we made our way down the corridor to the dining car, two boys dashed off to warn their parents of our approach. The latter jostled each other out of the compartment to come out and look at me, and the barbs of their sniggering looks dug deep into my flesh. We looked for a seat in the dirty, crowded dining car while the diners stopped eating to examine us from every angle.

We then realized how familiar we were with Indian cuisine. Probably because of our frequent dinners at Raj's. Although the menu was written in a vague attempt at English and comprising a great many Indian expressions, we recognized poppadums, samosas, chutney, chicken tandoori, chicken masala, chicken curry, biryani, payasam and other specials. There was one word, however, which turned up time and time again but which we were unable to decipher: Dal. Richard called the waiter and asked what it meant. The waiter, a fat man openly picking his teeth, almost burst out laughing.

'Dal is dal, sir,' he belched.

I picked up courage to order this strange dish. It turned out to be yellow lentils mashed into a puree which I had trouble swallowing.

Very soon the journey became quite painful. There had been a misunderstanding. The Indians were not my brothers. Why were they so curious about me? What were those rude looks blaming me for? The colour of my skin? Some who roared with laughter were blacker than me. The features of my face? The texture of my hair? I was at my wit's end, gradually losing confidence in myself and starting to harbour all kinds of inferiority complexes.

There were, of course, some magical moments. We had booked in to the Rambagh Palace Hotel in Jaipur, not far from Lilypool where the famous Gayatri Devi resided. One evening, the hotel gardens were cordoned off for a reception in honour of the princess Ashraf, sister to the shah of Iran. While we were standing on the terrace, the strains of a strange, melodious music floated dreamily to our ears. Men in dazzling white jodhpurs and sumptuous orange turbans that fluttered like wings around their heads passed us by, perched on elephants, followed by a procession of dancers, their wrists and ankles clasped by heavy silver bracelets.

There was also a visit to the Palace of the Winds set with a thousand windows that the naked eye was unable to grasp.

In New Delhi, the proud capital and masterpiece of English architect Edwin Lutyens, who had managed to blend modernity and traditional charm in his achievements, we were guests of Michel, a French friend of Raj's. He taught at the university and was married to an Indian Muslim by the name of Sarojini, whose dark shining eyes and hair were the colour of prunes. As soon as we were seated on the ottomans in lieu of chairs, I declared that our journey was turning into a nightmare.

'You didn't do your homework,' he said off-handedly which I found hurtful. 'You should have read *Homo Hierarchicus* over and over again. It explains everything. This society is based on a caste system, one of whose essential elements is skin colour. Add to that your features and your hair which are so different from the Indians' and you shouldn't be surprised how disconcerting you are to the man in the street. You're intelligent enough to understand that, aren't you?'

The tone of his voice irritated me. I reflected on his explanations but was hardly convinced.

'As for saying that this journey is a nightmare for you,' he resumed sharply, 'it's unthinkable when you are constantly surrounded by so many objects of beauty.'

'Exactly!' I exclaimed. 'How can a society produce so much beauty if it excludes the human element?'

'It doesn't exclude the human element,' he protested. 'It has a different notion of it from yours. That's all!'

His words seemed to avoid the issue, endeavouring to justify an argument which goes simply by the name of racism.

'Forgive us,' his wife whispered, taking me gently by the hand and leading me to the table.

She had cooked a traditional dish of lamb with spinach macerated in coconut milk. I couldn't swallow it. India remained stuck in my throat. In a photo taken at the time, I have hollowed cheeks and a haggard look. During those five weeks in India, I think I lost at least 5 kilos, since to stave off my hunger I ate only samosas and drank two or three glasses of lassi. In the evening, Michel and Sarojini took us to a concert of traditional dances. It was a magical moment: seeing the delicate steps of the female dancers, the quivering of their arms, the gracious dislocating movement of their neck and hearing the jingling of their bracelets. Unfortunately, on the way back, we met a group of Sikhs. I had learnt to dread their mocking aggressiveness. They roared with laughter at me and the echo rippling through the streets flew back at me with a deadly force. How could they reconcile their legendary spirituality and their opposition to the caste system with such brutal behaviour? Don't religious convictions transform the individual?

On the day of our departure, Sarojini, who had been upset by my lack of appetite, offered me a book: a hundred recipes of traditional Indian cuisine including fifty vegetarian recipes.

'You'll make them,' she smiled sadly, 'once you have forgotten all this.'

We kissed goodbye. The experiences I was going through were piling up between us, separating us and preventing us from becoming the friends we could have been. I was never to see Sarojini again, but I still have the book of recipes she gave me. I often leaf through it. It tells me how to make sweet-and-sour sauce, a mixture of honey and vinegar. It lists the Indians' favourite spices: turmeric, cumin, coriander and saffron, as well as the vegetables they like: okra (known as bhindi), eggplant and spinach. Nevertheless I have never been tempted to try out even one of these recipes. It will bring back too many memories I prefer to forget.

We resumed our gruelling journey. Several times Richard offered to cancel the trip and return to Paris. A kind of perverse masochism camouflaged as courage prevented me from accepting such a proposition. I insisted on continuing to the bitter end. I was little aware that the last weeks would be the most trying.

The Taj Mahal is an all-too-familiar sight. It pops up on postcards, cheap calendars and tourist brochures. But when you come face to face with the monument, you are overcome with a strange emotion. Why? Because of its extraordinary beauty? The purity of its architectural lines? Because Emperor Shah Jahan's power of love for his wife Mumtaz Mahal overwhelms us even today? Richard wandered off to take photos but I collapsed on one of the park benches. There I lay prostrate, crying perhaps, dreaming most probably. I remembered Michel's words: 'How can you say that this journey is a nightmare when India is packed with so many objects of beauty?' He was right. No other country had given me such a profusion of refinement. That was all that mattered. I was about to blame myself when a group of teenagers surrounded me, laughing, making faces and shouting a word I first had trouble deciphering. Then I understood: 'Monkey, monkey.' They were calling me a monkey. This racist insult dies hard since Christiane Taubira, the former French justice minister, had been spattered with it. The reactions it causes are complex. First, the victim feels pity for her aggressors: How could they be so stupid as to compare me to a monkey? she tells herself. Then emerges a raging anger. She wants to take revenge. She wants to stick this insult down the throat of her assailants. The anger then turns into helplessness, a feeling of vulnerability and fear. Do I really look like a monkey? the victim asks in dismay. I don't know for how long the crazed band of teenagers danced around me. Suddenly a khaki-uniformed armed squad wearing flat caps and wielding truncheons ran up and the teenagers scampered off.

'Did they attack you?' one of them asked. 'They're a bunch of hooligans who attack tourists. Yesterday they robbed several. You're lucky they didn't steal anything!'

I don't know how I managed to get to Varanasi. I was filled with insane expectations. Varanasi is the holy city beside the Ganges. The pilgrims who gather there must certainly be of another frame of mind from those who had already crossed my path. Their thoughts are surely only on prayer and communing with their god. Alas, it was nothing of the sort. The men and women standing up to their waist in the waters of the holy river interrupted their ritual ablutions to point at me and snigger. For me it was the last straw. From that moment on all I could think of was returning to Paris. Unfortunately, due to the crowds of pilgrims and tourists, no seat was available in the train back to Mumbai for at least a week. We had to resort to flying to Calcutta the day after. While I was slumped on a seat in the airport lounge, a group of young Indian nuns entered, forming a circle around a European woman who was obviously their Mother Superior. She must have been about sixty, with exquisite eyes, both sparkling and gentle under her white headscarf bordered with blue. She waved a friendly greeting and walked over to me. In my condition, I was in no fit state to cross swords with a nun. I couldn't help smiling in turn, however, and shook the hand she held out.

'Where do you come from in Africa?' she asked me in a gentle tone. 'We have a sister who comes from Namibia.'

I explained that I didn't come from Africa but from a small island, a long way away, called Guadeloupe.

'I have never been to the Caribbean,' she said. 'It's a pity. I dream of visiting Haiti. When you're in Calcutta,' she continued kindly, 'come and visit our orphanage and our home for the underprivileged. I'd like to see you again. There's so much misery in this country. We do all we can but it's just a drop in the ocean.'

Thereupon she handed me her business card. It was Mother Teresa whom at that time I had never heard of and who wasn't yet the icon she was to become. I did not respond to her kind invitation since I no longer had the strength. I was in a daze. During the three days we spent in Calcutta, I remained locked up in our hotel. I only came out in the evening, hugging the walls in the hope of going unnoticed, in order to buy samosas and cans of lassi from a small cafe selling takeaway food. Oddly enough, the inquisitiveness that had tortured me elsewhere was less evident in Calcutta. A cosmopolitan crowd filled the streets. The neon-lighted displays pierced the night. The bars remained wide open.

I was wild with joy at being back in Paris. No one looked at me. Nobody turned their head when I entered a bar or a restaurant and this blessed indifference which I was enjoying, far from nettling my feminine vanity, seemed wonderful. Richard, however, wrote to the Indian ambassador describing the way I had been treated throughout our stay. He did not ask for an apology (what use would it have been?) but insisted on conveying how hurt we had been. To our great surprise, the ambassador replied. He sent us a beautiful book illustrating the treasures of the maharajas' palaces with a long letter both dignified and compassionate. Although he deeply regretted the behaviour we complained about, India needed to be judged on another less superficial level: it was a non-aligned country that took an active part in the development of Africa and provided economic and political assistance in a host of circumstances. For example, it gave scholarships and grants to researchers and organized exchanges between universities. We should never forget that India was one of the leading lights of the Third World.

A few weeks later, we were invited by Raj for a chicken biryani. Strangely enough, my liking for Indian cuisine had come back, as if the hostility and ostracism of its inhabitants were the sole cause of my lack of appetite. I downed a glass of lassi with a kind of emotional gratitude.

'Why didn't you warn us?' I reproached him.

'I didn't have the courage,' he confessed. 'Richard and you were so excited. I knew you had read *Homo Hierarchicus* and that you were well aware of the caste system.'

I recovered from India quicker than I expected. The memory of the sniggers, sneers and insults faded and I recalled only the glimpses of beauty: the Taj Mahal, Fatehpur Sikri, Udaipur as well as the temples and palaces. There was one question, however, that I was dying to ask my many Indian friends whom I was later to meet in the US: Has India changed? Has the racism disappeared? If I'm reluctant to ask such a question, it's because after all it's absurd. It could be formulated more generally. I could ask whether the world has changed or whether racism still exists.

America, This Land Is Your Land,
This Land Is My Land,
This Land Was Made for You and Me

At the end of 1987, I received a letter from a certain Howard Bloch, head of the French Department at the University of Berkeley in California. Oddly enough he made no mention of my novel *Segu*, whose two volumes had been relatively successful and earned me numerous letters from readers. Rather, he went into raptures over *I, Tituba: Black Witch of Salem* which I had published the previous year. A Jew himself, he told me how much he had liked this provocative rewriting of an infamous episode in the history of the US as well as the satirical portrait of the relations between Jews and blacks. Consequently, he offered me a position as visiting professor for a semester. This was an unexpected delectable revenge since I had called upon Tituba, the slave originally from Barbados and accused of bewitching the little girls of Salem, in order to free me from the frustrations I had experienced three years earlier. Thanks to one of my admirers, Annabelle Rea, a Fulbright scholarship had allocated me a one-year teaching position at Occidental College, a small liberal arts college in Los

Angeles. It was there that Barack Obama had been an undergraduate. Unfortunately when I arrived, Obama was no longer a student and I spent a very unpleasant year.

I disliked Los Angeles immensely—a huge, sprawling city, a complicated tangle of highways and bridges covered by a grey fog of pollution that hung low and heavy like a lid. In order to get to the beaches of Santa Monica and Malibu, where the quality of air was somewhat better, you had to drive for hours amid a flow of cars. I adored the movies, but the Hollywood sign on one of the surrounding hills did nothing to make me dream. I was witness to a racism, not primitive or loud as in India, but silent, oppressive and pernicious. Apart from Annabelle, none of my colleagues spoke to me, none of my colleagues even looked at me. 'Invisible Woman', to parody Ralph Ellison, that's what I had become. I had no intention of repeating such an experience and so I put Howard Bloch's invitation, however flattering it may have been, away in a drawer.

I changed my opinion, however, and for a second time found myself back in America. It may surprise some people but I have never been victim to the myth of America. As a child I accompanied my brothers and sisters to the movies of Shirley Temple; despite my young age, I was hurt and irritated by the grotesque portrayal of blacks around her. In a film whose name I have forgotten, a black shoeshine boy asks stupidly: 'Why's they call a boot a boot, Miss Shirley?' Later, the image of blacks in *Gone with the*

Wind merely confirmed my distrust. Moreover, my intellectual guides depicted America as the den of capitalism, heaven on earth for the exploitation of man by man.

But ever since I had returned to Guadeloupe after the publication of *Segu*, declaring somewhat pompously that I was putting myself at the service of my island, nobody apparently needed my services. I was never invited to participate in something worthwhile and spent all my time on my balcony, writing works which nobody was interested in. When they passed by our front gate, my neighbours would peer up to take a look at 'The African'—as they called me since it was rumoured I was from Mali—busy with her futile scribbling. You could count the number of our visitors on your fingers. There was my brother and sister-in-law with one or several of their children who came to visit from Basse-Terre. We had nothing to say to each other; they didn't like my cooking but felt obliged to come by and be bored once a month. Our friend José, a militant for independence, came whenever the fancy took him in order to sell the party's newspaper. One day he brought along a frail, apparently shy mulatto, the Creole-speaking poet Sony Rupaire who was to become one of my best friends.

I also had no inclination to be separated from Richard for such a long period of time. He had found work of sorts, and, confronted with all manner of problems, taught translation within the context of vocational training.

Finally, I had absolutely no desire to leave Guadeloupe. By Guadeloupe I mean an entity I have trouble defining, such as the nature of the island—the sea, the beaches, the forests, banana groves and sugar-cane fields—not because of its beauty, spoilt year after year by the property developers, but because of a concert of subtle, faint voices it emitted for me alone. This concert irrigated my imagination and illuminated my thoughts.

Nevertheless, these excellent reasons didn't prevent me from leaving for Berkeley in January 1988. After almost two days of travelling—I had to change planes in Puerto Rico and Dallas—I arrived early evening at the airport in San Francisco, the closest to Berkeley, tired out and racked in deep depression. Bloch, who was to play a fundamental role in my university career in the US, was waiting for me at the airport. He took me for dinner at his place with his wife, Helen, and his numerous children. I found myself back again in the familiar atmosphere I had left behind in Paris: cheeky young things, always ready to contradict their parents or openly bored. It reassured me. We instantly became friends, Howard, Helen and I, a true family. However, I must have looked downhearted since Helen gently scolded me: 'Don't show that you're missing your husband. It's not the done thing here. Berkeley is a den of feminists.'

'And blue stockings,' Howard added.

I was in for a great surprise. Up till then I had always considered American cuisine a lost cause.

During my year in Los Angeles, all I had eaten were cheeseburgers, hamburgers and different sorts of sandwiches. In the Glendale district, where Annabelle Rea lived, I had discovered a chain of stores called Maria Callenda whose food, mainly pies, were fairly good. At Thanksgiving, Annabelle invited me to share a traditional meal at her house. Unfortunately, I found the main dish of turkey as tasteless as boiled cardboard and resorted to the side dishes of cranberries, Brussels sprouts and sweet-potato puree. That evening at Howard and Helen's house, Jewish cuisine came as a revelation. For the first time I tasted a delicious stew of potatoes, carrots and a cut of meat I had never used. But when I asked Helen for her recipes, she eluded the question. For her, cooking was not a secular distraction that anyone can appropriate. Cooking was conditioned by religion, traditions and shared ideas that I, as a non-Jew, could not partake in. I had to wait years, until I was living in New York and my friend Louise Yellin, who was more open-minded, gave me the recipes of Ashkenazi cuisine: *latkes*, grilled chicken liver and meat balls.

Howard's and Helen's warnings were to have little effect on me since I immediately fell in love with Berkeley. The first semester was pure delight. Not only did I never tire of admiring the campus with its centuries-old trees and flower beds but also I had never breathed in such an intellectual and enriching atmosphere. I was given free rein to organize my classes and to select and teach my favourite authors.

No boring homework, no tedious essays or grading. The most the students did was read the list of books and make oral presentations followed by a class discussion. My colleagues were charming and welcoming. I avoided three professors only: two men who lived together; and another who, it was whispered, was in love with a gas-station attendant in Castro, the homosexual neighbourhood in San Francisco. The word 'homosexuality' made me run for cover. These three men could well bring back a constant pain I was desperately trying to hide. After a difficult adolescence which had drained both of us, my son had told me he was gay. I had taken it very badly, I must admit. Mortified, he had left for Africa and I had no news of him. One of my sisters said he was in the Ivory Coast. Doing what exactly?

I could have been fully satisfied in Berkeley if I hadn't nurtured a dream that was dear to my heart. A great admirer of Martin Luther King Jr, I wanted to get to know and if possible integrate into the African American community. It had not been possible at Occidental College where, except for me, there was just one mixed-blood teacher from Louisiana who was seldom on campus since she was constantly invited elsewhere. At Berkeley there was a big department of African American studies and I was determined things would be different. Shortly after I arrived, I wrote a letter to the head of the department, a certain Mary Wallace, to ask for an appointment. My intentions, though, remained extremely confused. I was planning to speak about myself, get my writing known and possibly give two or three lectures on the literature of the French Antilles. Mary Wallace responded after a considerable delay of several weeks. We met for lunch at the Shattuck Hotel, an elegant building which prided itself on hosting visitors since the beginning of the century. It also boasted of its excellent cuisine, *real* Reuben and club sandwiches served with French fries.

Mary Wallace arrived flanked by a poet from Mississippi, oddly named Dorian Gray, who apparently was very famous. The two women talked together throughout the meal, virtually ignoring me. I was wondering why Mary Wallace had accepted my invitation when at 2.30 p.m. she and Dorian Gray got up and left. Mary Wallace promised to write me but never did. From that day on, whenever I met her on campus, flanked by the inevitable Dorian Gray, she would kiss me on both cheeks and call me sister but obviously had nothing to say to me. I ended up realizing I would never be integrated into the African American community. I spoke English with a French accent. My ancestors had never trembled during the terror of the KKK's lynching spree. Relatives and friends had never hung heavy like strange fruit from the branches of the trees in the South. My mother, dead tired, had never sat at the back of the bus nor been obliged to give up her seat to a white man. Once again, Negritude was fraying at the edges and showing its limitations. It didn't prevent me, however, from taking an interest in the activities of the Department of African American Studies. I attended the screening of two remarkable documentaries, one on Zora Neale Hurston, the other on Katherine Dunham. One afternoon, Alice Walker came and discussed *The Color Purple* to protests from a bunch of male chauvinists.

One evening, I was bold enough to push open the door of Martha's, a soul food restaurant in Oakland, the black city next door to Berkeley. Photos of famous African Americans beamed down from their frames in the large dining room: W. E. B. Du Bois, Martin Luther King Jr, Andrew Young, Jesse Jackson, Malcolm X and a host of others. A profound nostalgia made my heart bleed at the thought that any relation with them would be rejected: an impression that was made even more painful by the curious looks the customers gave me. I had time, however, to taste a dish which I thought unoriginal: fried chicken, somewhat brittle, black-eyed peas and sweet potatoes.

In order to get over these stinging disappointments, whenever I had time, I sat in on classes of Chicano studies, as the countless Mexicans were called who were born and grew up in California. Very soon I became friends with Maria Azzaro who taught anthropology. Despite her young age—she was barely thirty—she had a strong personality and was twice divorced. She had made no bones about leaving her only son with his father for fear he would hamper her career, something I would have been incapable of doing. We were worlds apart but I deeply admired her intelligence and her beauty. When we were together, we were not merely content to discuss Octavio Paz's book *The Labyrinth of Solitude* or Gloria Anzaldua's brilliant theories on borderlands. United by a common passion for cooking, we scoured the numerous Mexican restaurants in Berkeley, San Francisco and Sausalito. On weekends, we cooked at her place or mine. I preferred her place, since the food tastes better when there is a large gathering of guests and at her house there were always loads of cousins, nephews and nieces who munched on tacos and tortillas amid the smell of reheated cooking fat. Once a month, her mother arrived from Sacramento, loaded with baskets of ingredients. She then proceeded to give us a genuine cooking demonstration. One day, she even attempted to dig a hole in the middle of the azaleas in the garden for she was determined to cook a cochinita pibil, a mixture of pork and all kinds of vegetables.

'You have to cook it in banana leaves,' Maria kept saying, exasperated.

Her mother took no notice since she had brought with her an ample provision of foil. In the end, banana leaves or foil, the cochinita pibil turned out to be delicious although a bit too spicy for my taste. I hate hot pepper—it burns the mouth and deadens the subtlety of flavours.

Maria's relationship with her mother helped me considerably to imagine how my own mother related to my grandmother Victoire. It helped me write my novel *Victoire, My Mother's Mother*. In fact Maria worshipped her mother who, after her husband had been killed in mysterious circumstances, perhaps drug-related, had bravely raised her daughter on her miserable wages as a cook in a restaurant. At the same time she quarrelled with her since she was ashamed of her ignorance. After over thirty years of living in the States, her mother couldn't speak a word of English nor did she know the name of the president. Maria held her jealousy and possessiveness partly responsible for the failure of her two marriages.

Maria's favourite dish was albondigas, spicy meat balls served with rice. One lunch time I timidly asked her permission to cook a mole de Puebla. I loved this strange dish, a blend of very bitter plain chocolate and very sweet dried fruit.

'You are gifted,' Maria admitted after several mouthfuls. 'During the summer holidays, I'll have to take you to my grandmother in Cuernavaca. It's her speciality.'

No other comment could have flattered my ego.

It was then that a Martinican professor, Beatrice Mole, invited me to give a lecture on Césaire's *Notebook of a Return to the Native Land* at Tulane University where she taught. I'd like to take this opportunity to point out how much Césaire's reputation in the States is owed to the few French Antilleans who were teaching there at the time. Up till 1950, his name was vaguely familiar to a handful

of intellectuals who had seldom read his work.
Thanks to us, *Notebook of a Return to the Native
Land*, *Discourse on Colonialism* and *The Dogs Were
Silent* are now given pride of place in the depart-
ments of francophone literature.

Tulane University is located in New Orleans.
New Orleans! I did not even dream of refusing such
an invitation. The mere name conjures up so many
legends: the birth of jazz, the homeland of Louis
Armstrong and Cajun music, culinary marvels, mysterious bayous. I was prepared to cross the entire
country to get there. At the time, all I knew of the US
was California and two cities of opposites: Los
Angeles, an urban megalopolis where the automobile
reigns supreme; and San Francisco, traversed by the
fragrance of the winds and open to the high seas.
Later I was often invited to New Orleans and it
became almost familiar.

One day the nuns from Xavier, the Catholic University, invited me for a memorable breakfast on the
banks of the Mississippi. Two of my plays were performed there in a university setting: *The Tropical
Breeze Hotel* directed by a Nigerian, Akin Euba; and
Like Two Brothers directed by the Martinican, José
Exelis.

I shall never forget how amazed I was on my first
visit to New Orleans. It was not just the arrogant
beauty of the city that struck me with its elegant
houses dating back to its past history of slavery, the
surprising exoticism of the French Quarter or the

splendour of the wide, tree-lined avenues. It was first and foremost the skin colour of its inhabitants. Although the African Americans constituted a large minority in California, they remained mostly in the ghettos and seldom left their black neighbourhoods. In New Orleans, they were everywhere, they filled the streets and the pavements, the buses and the trams with their exuberant presence. You could have been in Pointe-à-Pitre or Basse-Terre.

Beatrice Mole, who was waiting for me at the airport, was a very pretty high yellow girl in spite of a face spotted with freckles, as if she had looked at the sun through a sieve.

'It's a completely different kind of America,' I said excitedly. 'You're so lucky to live here.'

'I would prefer to live in Castro.'

'Castro?'

Her expression hardened. 'I'm gay. I'm living with another woman, Cassia. You can't imagine how narrow-minded the African American community is. They loathe us and we have no friends.'

I was shattered. Homosexuality again? Couldn't it leave me in peace? I could cross seas and oceans and it would still haunt me. In the taxi that took us to the bed and breakfast where a room had been booked for me and then on to Beatrice's, my ears were ringing. My heart was pounding. That's why New Orleans for me wasn't simply a centre of gastronomy, the city of donuts and the French Quarter, the queen of crawfish casserole and gumbo stew, those dishes the slaves brought with them when their masters were chased out of Haiti at the end of the eighteenth century. I never went to eat at Galatoire's, the place to be seen in for the city's high society dressed in all its finery and wearing wide-brimmed hats to lunch on crab Sardou. New Orleans for me is where the suffering deep inside me once again flooded my heart.

Beatrice Mole lived in the last house at the end of a remote street at the back of a garden that was a true tangle of azaleas and rhododendrons. At the end of the day, Cassia, her partner, drove up on a red, sputtering motorbike. I must confess she was not lacking for charm, an appealing blend of coquetry and innocence. The two women kissed each other passionately. I couldn't help averting my eyes and at once I was ashamed of myself. At my age, was I such a prude? We sat round a frugal dinner of pumpkin soup and chocolate cake. When we had finished, I was somewhat shocked when Beatrice threw her arms around Cassia. Snuggled against her shoulder, Cassia began to dream.

'You come from the Caribbean, don't you? I would love to live in Martinique, in Le François for example, in a small house on the edge of the sea. We would live off sea urchin blaffs and fresh fish.'

'Don't be silly,' Beatrice gently interrupted her. 'In Martinique, the people are worse. People from the Caribbean don't want to confront homosexuality. Frantz Fanon went so far as to deny its very existence in our islands. It's far from the truth. Everywhere in the working-class districts, women live together. They're called *zanmi*. Audrey Lorde talks about them in her remarkable book.'

I had nothing to say since, however hard I searched my memory, I could remember nothing of the kind. Homosexuality in Guadeloupe? All I could recall were men disguised crudely as women during carnival and the insult *makoumé* that was thrown at them.

The following day, during my presentation on Césaire, a group of African American students arrived on a bus from the university at Baton-Rouge to add a dissenting voice. They didn't care two hoots about Césaire whom they probably had never read. What they were contesting was the image of Africa I had depicted in *Segu*. For three years I had been blamed for the same things. I had not condemned female genital mutilation. The character of Malobali gave the impression that all Africans were drunkards or rapists. The lovemaking of Tiekoro and Nadié as they sailed down the Joliba gave the impression that all Africans were filled with lust. I was starting to get used to such nonsense and soon got the upper hand over my opponents.

The dinner at Beatrice's was just as frugal as the day before: a four-vegetable soup and a fruit cake. While we were sharing dessert, Cassia turned to me and wanted to know whether a writer was obliged to depict real life. Didn't she have the right to distort it? Or tone it down or embellish it so that her readers can dream and face reality? In short, she was wondering whether a writer shouldn't be, first and foremost, a purveyor of myths. Perhaps she was right. But I knew only how to dip my pen in the ink of truth. Beatrice caressed her again which made me feel uncomfortable.

'She's asking you these questions,' she said, 'because she dreams of becoming a novelist.'

'I'm already on page fifty of my first novel,' Cassia explained. 'But I'm wondering whether my nationality is not a handicap. As a Chilean, I'm expected to keep trotting out the coup d'état by Pinochet, the death of Allende, the disappearance of so many patriots. I'm not ashamed to confess that those things don't interest me at all. All I want to portray is how my love for Beatrice has brought magic into my life.'

A Sapphic novel, I thought contemptuously. Influenced by Gilberto Freyre, I believed a novel should raise the reader's conscience.

'Whatever!' Beatrice exclaimed delighted and embraced her. 'All that counts is the freedom of the artist.'

The discussion stopped there. I soon took my leave since Beatrice and Cassia had begun to fondle each other and visibly desired to be left alone. That night, back in my room, Beatrice's affirmation turned over and over again in my mind. What did she mean? Was the writer free to say anything to her readers?

Was she obliged to shock them? Shouldn't writing comprise a certain dose of self-censorship?

I spent my last morning admiring the Great Houses of the American and French planters between New Orleans and Baton Rouge. The Americans' were more spectacular, genuine temples to Mammon embellished with majestic porches and colonnades. Some had been opened as museums where crowds of tourists aimed their cameras at everything. I tried to imagine these places swarming with slaves, busy satisfying their masters' whims, cooking meals or painfully picking cotton under the searing sun. But the emotion wasn't there. As I have said, since my parents never talked to me about slavery, I had little thoughts of tenderness or nostalgia for the suffering of my ancestors. I accepted the offer by Christian Paul, then minister in the Lionel Jospin government in France, to become president of the Committee for the Memory of Slavery created after the publication of the Taubira Law, precisely because it was intended to make amends for this guilty omission and make up for this shocking lack of compassion.

Back in Berkeley I dragged Maria to Castro, the neighbourhood I had always obliterated from my mind because, although I knew it to be a Mecca for homosexuals the world over, I refused to look this painful reality straight in the eye. I had great trouble managing to convince her since she was terrified we would be taken for lesbians.

'What does it matter?' I joked.

'You're crazy!' she exclaimed, staring at me horrified.

I must confess that at first I felt uncomfortable among all these same-sex couples smoking, chattering, laughing and dancing, clasped in each other's arms, in places reserved exclusively for them. I was not bigoted enough to condemn them but they bothered me. Gradually, I began to realize that they were protecting themselves from the very same people who hunted and terrorized blacks and Jews. Gradually, I began to realize that, in their own way, homosexuals were warriors fighting for a certain kind of freedom.

A certain kind of freedom? Can you carve freedom up into slices? No, it is one and indivisible.

When I returned to New Orleans, Cassia and Beatrice were living in a women's colony in Vermont. I kept up a correspondence with Beatrice. A few years later she told me that she and Cassia had a daughter, Laurence. It was Cassia who had borne her and her pregnancy had been the result of an artificial insemination. Such an event no longer smacked of science fiction to me, and I was no longer shocked. I had finally acknowledged the world had changed. When I was young, women were scared that their lovemaking would turn into unwanted motherhood. Today they were capable of having a child whenever they wanted, without direct intervention from a man. Beatrice, however, never mentioned again the novel that Cassia had undertaken. I concluded that Cassia had preferred a creation of the flesh rather than of imagination. She probably thought it a more reliable choice.

At the end of the semester in Berkeley, Howard offered me tenure. It was a masterly stroke of good fortune! I nevertheless requested a few days to think it over. For me, making a choice comes down to giving up other possibilities, closing the door on other prospects. I was not prepared to spend the rest of my life in the States. Admittedly, in Guadeloupe, I lived in splendid isolation, even exclusion you might say. When I went to sign my books at Jasor's, the main bookstore on the island, I was merely following a vain ritual. Nobody was really interested in my work. And yet, as I have said, this was not the essential element. I maintained a beloved dialogue with the entire island. Early morning, before switching on my computer, I opened my bedroom windows on the foothills of La Soufrière still clothed in mist . . . I can remember the marvellous feeling it aroused in me. Should I give it all up?

While I was hesitating, Howard was running out of patience. 'I would like your answer before the end of the month,' he said.

In order to play for time, I replied I was waiting to hear what my husband thought.

Of course, I ended up accepting his offer. To celebrate the occasion, we uncorked a few bottles of champagne at Howard's with Helen and one of their friends, Leo Feldman. This eighty-year-old Jew was full of anecdotes. Chased out of Germany, he had landed in New York with his family between the two wars. Thanks to his father, who had made his fortune making mother-of-pearl buttons in Brooklyn, he had been able to study biology, become a famous scientist and almost won a Nobel Prize.

Unfortunately, Howard left Berkeley to head the French Department at Columbia University in New York. He later managed to have me appointed to Columbia, but, at the very moment I arrived, he left to teach at Yale. Richard came to join me in Berkeley in July and we set up the life we would now lead: spend Christmas and summer holidays in Guadeloupe, and the rest of the year in the US, not to mention the visits to Richard's parents in the UK. We managed to keep to this somewhat complicated agenda up to 2007.

When Richard came to join me, it was summer in a California filled with multicoloured, sweet-smelling flowers. We both fell in love with the region that was so lovely and so varied. We spent two days in Yosemite Natural Park measuring the trunks of the giant sequoias and kayaking up the rivers.

Alas, I was not to stay long in Berkeley since all those who were dear to me left one after the other. In the fall of 1989, Maria Azzaro accepted an invitation to teach at Yale.

'I'll have you come to Yale,' she promised on the last evening as we dined at her place. 'You and Richard, you'll give a presentation on the complex relation between author and translator. We should call it . . . What should we call it?' she mused.

'Intimate Enemies,' I suggested.

After bitter discussions with my editors, Richard, in fact, had become my English translator. But Maria never organized this presentation; it was given years later at Columbia. She only taught for one year at Yale since an obscure college in Maine offered her a small fortune to head its anthropology department.

That's typical of American universities. Professors move around, depending on the type of attractive or prestigious offer they receive. They have little feeling of belonging to a particular location. I too succumbed to this contagion and sold myself to the highest bidder right up to 1995 when I was appointed by Howard to Columbia. Together with Richard, I moved from the University of Virginia campus in Charlottesville to Maryland's at College Park, then onto Harvard in Cambridge. The reason I regret the prestigious university of Harvard is not because of its setting, a series of austere, heavy brick buildings, nor because of its excellent students, little informed of francophone literature, nor because of the intellectual quality of my colleagues who were often remarkable leading lights in their subject. It's because there is an exquisite culinary speciality in Boston owing to its proximity to the ocean. There's a season when crabs moult their exoskeleton and the shell becomes tender and edible. Soft-shell crabs do not need to be garnered with spices—lemon juice and a little melted butter suffice.

THE TASTE OF TOKYO

Nothing had prepared me for New York. For almost ten years, I had lived in small-town America where the university governed the routine from morning to night. All the towns looked like poor copies of Edward Hopper's paintings. A series of haberdasher stores, a drugstore and supermarket lined Main Street, not to mention a bar always crowded as soon as night fell. It was intersected at regular intervals by side streets lined with identical houses. In winter, the front yards were white with snow. In summer, washing billowed on lines. Three times a week, I taught classes that I had meticulously prepared during long hours in a library filled with studious and silent students. In my free time I would write my novels. I was so absorbed by the world I was writing that I was totally unaware of what was going on around me. I was oblivious to the dull skies, the frost and even perhaps the snow that was falling. I was unaware of time passing.

Richard, working on his translations in the next room, would burst into my office: 'I'm starving!' he'd exclaim. 'Do you realize what time it is?'

Ashamed, I would dash into the kitchen and quickly cook something for lunch: nothing grandiose or fancy, we reserved that for dinner.

Evenings were somewhat limited. Sometimes I would listen to lecturers from other universities, sometimes attend concerts performed by the university's music department. Whenever there was a cine-club, it would take preference, even though it screened old films I had already seen. Nothing was organized on Sundays, so that professors with small children could take them to the ever-popular baseball game. Sunday evenings were occupied by invitations to dinner. Since there was no serious competition, my dinners had the reputation of being the best for miles around. People would fight to get invited.

Suddenly everything changed. I found myself in a city that never sleeps. Night was as noisy as day: ambulances screaming, police cars wailing, cars honking and the hum of pedestrians. I was dazzled by an unimaginable wealth and diversity of culture. How could one possibly choose between all the musicals, operas, plays, ballets and films? The most famous presenters, novelists and poets presided in venues where crowds lined up for hours to listen to them. Columbia University had long remained outside this intellectual hubbub since it is situated in Morningside Heights, on the borders of Harlem which put the fear of God into many. When I came to live there in 1995, Rudy Giuliani had already completed his safety operations and the neighbourhood was no longer a scaremonger. All kinds of businesses flowed in, forcing out the original Jewish population and making way for a series of sparkling new stores. In the narrow perimeter around the building where we lived were two Chinese restaurants, a French brasserie, a Korean restaurant, a Ghanaian restaurant, two Indian restaurants, two Japanese restaurants and four Italian restaurants, not to mention the countless fast food shops such as McDonald's, Pizza Hut and KFC which were mushrooming just about everywhere. Further down, towards 110th Street, were Thai restaurants, a Turkish restaurant where young beauties performed belly dancing, as well as an Afghan restaurant. At Rosita's, a Cuban restaurant, Richard and I ate a delicious meal in the company of René Depestre who had come to present his collection of poems, *Poète à Cuba*.

It was in New York that I became convinced that it is neither possible nor desirable to compete with traditional cuisines, *stricto sensu*. We should invent, reinvent according to our taste, and recreate according to our imagination. In cuisine, every daring invention is permitted. I keep in mind the delightful memory of a Thanksgiving dinner with my American friends where I replaced the mandatory turkey with a goose marinated in orange juice and aged rum. My guests were overjoyed. Henceforth my inventiveness knew no limits.

However, little did I know that my books were making their own sweet way. A Japanese translator in Seattle by the name of Suga had somehow come across my latest novel, *Tree of Life*, a work of fiction about my father's social ascension, and was determined to translate it. He had therefore requested the association of French professors to invite me to Tokyo for their annual meeting so that I could be introduced to Japanese scholars. Let there be no mistake: I was a nonentity. Since the annual assembly was focused on Marcel Proust, the guest of honour was an Oxford don who had written extensively on *Remembrance of Things Past*. I was to make my presentation before the closing remarks of the colloquium. Despite these reservations, I was overjoyed and proud to be invited to Japan. Having lived three years in Berkeley, I was well aware of the country's cultural riches. Since my articulations had begun to pain me, especially my right knee, I had undergone several sessions of shiatsu, the famous Japanese massage. Afterwards I would go to a traditional restaurant where the dishes revolved on a small train around a long table—the art consisted of grabbing what you fancied as it rolled by. I was not very good at this exercise in acrobatics and regularly spilt the little sushi or sashimi boats to the great glee of the other customers.

I had also read numerous Japanese writers: Mishima obviously, Abe Kobo, Kawabata, Shusaku Endo, Murakami, Oe and many others. Once my invitation was confirmed, I delved into rereading *A Barbarian in Asia* by Henri Michaux. The Barbarian was me, I thought proudly.

Richard and I landed at Narita airport late one afternoon but were incapable of knowing for certain whether it was the day before or after we had left JFK. Nobody was waiting for us. First, because I was not important enough; and second, because the airport was located too far from Tokyo. For almost two hours, a minibus drove us along a road bordered by a thick vegetation of strange trees. The trees in Japan are magnificent. I don't know where Michaux was looking when he wrote: 'The trees are sickly, puny, meager, rising feebly, growing with difficulty, fighting against adversity, and tortured as soon as possible by man in order to appear still more dwarfish and miserable.'

Quite the opposite. The foliage along the road leading to the city was so dense that Sleeping Beauty could have stayed asleep for three hundred years. I don't know how we managed to find our hotel, since the driver left us on an esplanade next to an impenetrable park. As he didn't speak a word of a foreign language, he merely gestured in the direction we should take. Our hotel room was comfortable but we were so excited that we decided to go out and explore.

From that first evening Tokyo terrified me in a way I had never been before. Tokyo was too immense, too crowded, teeming with hordes of pedestrians who, when the lights turned green, crossed the streets and the avenues in a disciplined surge. The night was violently illuminated by the neon lights and yet I was unable to decipher neither the signs nor the billboards. They were written in characters that made no sense to me. It was as if I was walking in a hostile, repelling environment. I couldn't help remembering an African story I had heard called 'The Monstrous Baby': In a village in the Sahel, a woman gave birth to a baby boy. Barely had he emerged from his mother's womb than he chased away the midwife and relatives come to help. Then, standing on his own two legs, he began to bellow for food. Since his mother was incapable of procuring any, he strangled her in rage. Just as the child kills its mother, so too the city kills the individual. Emperor Meiji in his wildest dreams could never have imagined that one day the conventional Edo would be transformed into this Tokyo.

Around midnight we entered a restaurant that was packed with customers who began to give us sidelong glances their whispers soon turning to smiles and nods. Since we were unable to decipher the menu, the waiter chose for us: two bowls of soup and two dishes of peas mixed with green beans and slices of black radish. Then two plates of chicken on a skewer which I learnt later was chicken yakitori. At the end of the meal, looking very pleased with himself, as if it were a great joke, he brought us a bottle of JM aged rum from Martinique. I, who didn't like rum very much, was dumbfounded. Richard and I drank to the health of the other customers who were only too keen to dispense with their sake. Since they spoke neither French nor English, we were greeted once again with a multitude of smiles and nods. Totally drunk, we took over an hour to find our hotel again. At the reception was a note in impeccable French informing us that a certain Chikako Mori had come to take us to dinner and would come by the following morning at 8.30 a.m. to guide us to the conference. Chikako Mori? Was it a boy or a girl? She turned out to be a girl, very young, very pretty, with a creamy complexion and drooping eyelids over sparkling eyes. Over a coffee in the hotel's dining room she explained, once again in polished French, that she was affiliated to the École de hautes études en sciences sociales in Paris and was writing her thesis on the speech used by the youth from the French suburbs. She held forth with great authority on an infamous Paris suburb where neither Richard nor I had set foot. It was surrealistic.

She then guided us through the maze of the Tokyo subway until we reached the venue of the annual meeting of French professors. Exhausted with jet lag and a virtually sleepless night, I fell asleep. The conference took place in a vast amphitheatre and was as solemn as a high mass, with the Oxford don and the Japanese professors filing one after the other onto the podium.

At the end of the afternoon, two young women summed up the conference deliberations in fancy French. While everyone jostled towards the exit, Chikako had us climb up to the fourth floor to a small room filled with young students. Space was limited, so some were sitting on the floor. Others were crowded in front of the wide-open windows for the heat was unbearable. No air-conditioning on the fourth floor, no interpretation equipment either. I had to speak in French. The interpreter beside me constantly interrupted me to ask for explanations. When I had finished speaking as best I could, two young girls, one with hair dyed ginger, the other green, collected and then translated questions from the audience which I endeavoured to answer. This went on for hours. Yet despite the amateurism and cumbersomeness of the encounter, I had a feeling of profound satisfaction. I felt I had achieved one of the essential functions of literature—to share a culture with individuals who are far removed from it. We carried out a transfer of identity. These young Japanese, spoilt children of the Pacific, set their pride to one side and emerged from their splendid isolation. Their shoulders bore the triple weight of dispossession, dispersion and exile of the people from the Caribbean. They discovered the plantation system where they were whipped by their cruel masters. They became the wretched of the earth.

While we followed Chikako for dinner, I discovered behind the noisy, brilliantly illuminated highways and avenues a stream of tangled alleyways lined with flower-bedecked little gardens, restaurants and tiny bars. The students who brought up the rear surrounded us as if we were stars, outdoing each other in politeness. One of them gave us the address of a blind shiatsu masseuse, the best you could find. Another offered to show us the temples in the area. Another even proposed driving us to the Golden Pavilion, made famous by Mishima.

Chikako introduced us to a tall young man in whom my expert Antillean eye detected a trace of black blood. His name was Michael Ferrier and was her partner. The other man beside Chikako introduced himself as Nobutaka Miura. 'My name is too long,' he smiled. 'Simply call me Nobu. This is my wife, Makiko.'

Nobu was a professor at the University of Chuo. For one trimester every year, he taught Japanese culture at the Université des Antilles-Guyane in Martinique, and was fully conversant with the writers of Créolité. So I was back to square one: I had travelled halfway round the world only to find myself back in the fold. Chikako took charge of ordering for us. That's how we came to taste vegetable and shrimp tempura, then beef teriyaki and black mushrooms. In Japan, the portions are so small you can keep on helping yourself as much as you like.

Chikako, Michael, Nobu and Makiko immediately became our close friends. We often meet up in Tokyo, Guadeloupe, Paris and New York. I invited Michael to Columbia University for a conference on orality and writing and he gave a remarkable presentation on Louis Ferdinand Céline. Since then he has become a well-known writer, notably the author of an excellent book on the Fukushima catastrophe.

Makiko, Nobu's wife, wrote a book inspired by her numerous visits to the Antilles and the wonder of the islands: *Martinique mon amour*.

I shall not describe in detail the commonplace tourist attractions of this first visit to Japan. We visited all the temples in the region, standing petrified with admiration in front of the statues of Buddha, some of whom were several metres high. We were captivated by the harmony of the zen gardens. Nobu took us to Hakone to give us a glimpse of pre-Westernized Japan: houses with sliding walls made of paper, bare rooms with no furniture, tatamis and communal baths with water heated to 42 degrees Centigrade.

One evening, we attended a Noh performance. To my great surprise, from the very start, half the spectators seemed to be asleep. I wondered if what looked like sleep wasn't in fact a kind of extreme concentration. But that I shall never know. For a long hour I was bored, running over and over in my head the academic essays I had read, all of which portrayed Noh as the quintessence of theatre. The actors, in long, floating robes and perched on wooden-soled sandals, fluttered about the stage, uttering sounds ranging from piercing shrieks to hoarse growls and mumblings. What was it all about? On our way out I asked Nobu who too seemed to have sunk into apparent sleep. He had his head deep in a map, since everyone who drives a car, even the taxi drivers, tries to find his way through the maze of streets, alleyways and dead ends.

'You didn't like it?' he asked absentmindedly.

'I didn't understand a word.'

'Tomorrow,' he promised, 'I'll bring you a book that will explain everything.'

He never did, and Noh remains one of my greatest cultural enigmas.

Two things remain important to me. One: the feeling that never left me of constantly being afraid in Tokyo and elsewhere in Japan. I don't know whether the word 'afraid' is appropriate. Perhaps I should borrow the expression of Michel Butor's, another frequent visitor to the Empire of the Rising Sun, of 'paralysing intimidation'. Not the fear of criminal violence. Rather, a feeling that originated from being aware that I was different. I had no right to fathom this thousand-year-old civilization. I was not in my rightful place, me, descendant of a slave, granddaughter of Caliban-Cannibal. I had brought about an inversion of the mirror image: a genuine upheaval.

Two: Japanese cuisine. I love it but it's the only one I have never attempted to imitate or interpret. Because in Japan eating is also an aesthetic act. Common ingredients of the daily routine must be dressed up. To fashion beetroot, cucumber, red cabbage, seaweed or mushrooms into unusual shapes elevates their status. Even the rice served in small quantities becomes an object of esteemed ornamentation. The notion of satiety which is fundamental to the act of eating is relegated to second place. In his *Empire of Signs*, Roland Barthes explains this in intellectual terms: 'The entire process of alimentation being in the composition, by composing your choices, you yourself make what it is you eat.'

You have to be a remarkable painter to elaborate still lifes from life itself. I am fully aware of my limitations, and I know I have no gift for the visual arts. As a devoted admirer, my mother would collect and frame my childhood drawings: shacks along the seashore under a circular sun, sailboats sailing over a blue, blue sea, etc. I cannot detect the slightest artistic talent in these childish sketches. As a result, if ever I thought of trying my hand at Japanese cuisine, I would mutilate it.

At the end of our third or fourth stay in Tokyo, we spent our last days at the home of Nobu and Makiko in the elegant district of Yoyogi-Shihuya. As is often the case in Tokyo, their apartment was small and cluttered with rugs, pictures and objects. Fortunately, there was a guest room which Nobu had fitted out for his mother who was now too ill and lived in a home for seniors. They invited Michael and Chikako to join us for a memorable farewell dinner. Everyone drank a great deal of sake, except me. Nobu knew I had a liking for champagne and had bought a bottle of Bollinger at an outrageous price. The dining table was covered with small red-lacquered bowls filled with all sorts of vegetables cut in diagonals, squares and diamonds. The centrepiece held a magnificent caramel-coated fish. There were also several varieties of tempura, some brown, some bright yellow, some scarlet. Once she had served the rice, as white as the teeth of a pretty woman goes the proverb from Guadeloupe, Makiko set down skewers of an especially savoury meat which I was unable to put a name to. Such a virtual mystical moment of communion was characteristic of what Japan had to offer. It mattered little that I had never tasted anything quite the same. The memory of that meal was to haunt me for the rest of my life.

This stay strengthened our ties with Mitsu, a Japanese friend, and his French wife, Noëlle, who taught francophone literature at the New School in New York. We made a point of scouring the Japanese restaurants in Manhattan but never again did I taste the magic I had experienced at our friends' place in Tokyo. Ironically, when Mitsu came for dinner to my apartment, he would demand and wolf down 'my callaloo', inspired by the memory of Adélia and her directives, but above all from what I had learnt during a stay in Benin. My callaloo was a not-very-attractive mixture of okra, spinach, salt pork and shrimps. The fact that it was Mitsu's favourite proves that the palate knows no nationality.

I returned to Japan five or six times, I think. Besides the translation of *Tree of Life*, thanks to Nobu and some other professors, several of my novels have been translated into Japanese: *I, Tituba*; *Tales from the Heart*; and *Windward Heights*. I was invited to speak through an interpreter at several universities. Unfortunately, it must be said that francophone Caribbean literature has not taken root in Japan. Except for Césaire, a beacon of light, it has never interested more than a handful of intellectuals who considered it a succulent curiosity. Although numerous students have written their doctoral thesis on my work, my books don't sell in Japan, a fact I deeply regret.

CUBA LIBRE

Tituba was no way prepared to let go. Although in the French-speaking world it was *Segu*, the story of the downfall of the Bambara kingdom situated in present-day Mali, which attracted a great many readers as well as a certain press, in other countries this diabolical witch exercised her ample charms. For those of you who haven't read the book, Tituba was a real person, a slave from Barbados who found herself caught up in the so-called witch trials of Salem near Boston. We know very little about her. Because of her status as a slave, she was not executed but sent to jail where she spent many long years. She was then sold but to whom we don't know. This scarcity of historical information allowed me to give full rein to my imagination. I endowed Tituba with a life of pure fantasy, and made her into a heroine like Nanny of the Maroons in Jamaica or the Mulâtresse Solitude in Guadeloupe.

I can understand why the American universities were bewitched by her charms, since they were given full backing by Angela Davis. In fact, her friend Howard Bloch had given her a copy of my book in French, a language she was fully conversant with.

She had liked it so much that she wrote a brilliant, though to my thinking slightly too militant, preface for the American translation. She had seen in Tituba a woman eclipsed by history because of her ethnic origins and social status. I would have liked her to highlight Tituba's provocative love stories as well as the deliberate anachronisms, such as the encounter with Hester Prynne in prison and the reflections on feminism. The success of Tituba in other countries never failed to surprise me. In the same year, I was invited to talk about her in places as different and distant as Cuba and Israel. I discovered, that despite their ideological differences, Israel and Cuba had a surprising number of points in common: both were home to a welcoming population with enquiring minds and interested in literature.

I was twenty at the time of the Cuban Revolution. The saga of the Barbudos, heroes of the Sierra Maestra, danced before my eyes and Fidel Castro was one of my idols. One of my most notable memories dates back to a visit by Che Guevara to the Winneba Ideological Institute while I was living in Accra. His handsome looks and long curly hair swept me off my feet. On a more serious note, in four hours, he presented a version of the socialist world where there would be neither oppressor nor oppressed; all would be united in the interest of the humble at heart. Later I heard and read numerous criticisms, some often caustic, of the Castro regime. They never managed to sway my convictions and I kept my faith intact in the Cuban Revolution.

It may seem surprising but I wasn't very enthusiastic about the Casa de Las Americas' invitation. But, since it was for the month of February, how could I possibly not exchange the cold in New York for the warmth and sensuality of the Caribbean? First, like all true lovers of New York, I was partial to the city in winter when it becomes grandiose. Christmas decorates its squares, gardens and streets with fir trees whose branches sag under the weight of their many-coloured lights. Sometimes a thick mantle of snow covers its streets. The billboards advertising musicals light up the night, crowded with lively and enthusiastic theatregoers. Everywhere the air seems more piquant and vibrant, stimulating the senses.

Second, it is not easy to travel to Cuba from the United States. We had to get up at dawn to board the flight from Toronto to Havana. The airport in Toronto is huge and I remember navigating endless corridors for hours before reaching our gate. We arrived in Havana early afternoon. After a ruthless interrogation by the immigration officers, two smiling and welcoming representatives from Casa de Las Americas greeted us in the arrival hall and guided us to a taxi. I had forgotten the virulence of the sun, the white clouds scooting across a metallic blue sky and that treacherous heat which seemed to penetrate right to the bone.

Throughout my stay in Cuba, I was constantly disconcerted by the mix of the familiar and unfamiliar. For instance, the two representatives from Casa de Las Americas resembled two mulattos from Guadeloupe. Yet their manners were far more enthusiastic and fraternal. I suddenly realized that this little girl with ribbons in her hair, walking wistfully to school hand in hand with an adult, was not in fact me. Although the bougainvillea and crotons lining the road into town were the same as those in Montebello or Capesterre-Belle-Eau, they were radiated by what seemed a brighter sun. Vintage American cars, Plymouths, Dodges, Studebakers and Chevrolets, transformed the streets into a 1950s Hollywood studio. Yet I felt in familiar territory since such images were straight out of the movies.

We were housed in the El Presidente hotel, a palace dating back to the 1920s, now rather shabby. The representatives from Casa de Las Americas accompanied us to the dining room. It was crowded with tourists which surprised me for I was unaware that, despite the American embargo, Cuba received so many visitors. Several tables were occupied by a noisy soccer team from Venezuela. I think I have never eaten so badly in all my life: an insipid vegetable soup, a tasteless chicken and brittle, crumbly plantain fries. Even the coffee didn't find favour with me: rather than a weak kiololo, it turned out to be a brownish liquid with an indefinable aroma. When we tried to go up to our room, we found the lifts to be out of order. We had to wait over an hour on the hotel's terrace before the technicians finished their repairs. I couldn't help notice the coming and going of several young girls, teenagers almost, and their posturing around the tourists. What did they want? Their behaviour was extremely provocative.

All these inconveniences were quickly forgotten once we entered the auditorium of Casa de Las Americas, situated close by and opposite the Malecon, the avenue that runs along the edge of the sea. It was packed with an audience containing every colour: blacks, mulattos and whites, which was surprising considering that, in Guadeloupe, unless they were from metropolitan France, the white Creoles always kept to themselves. Young people rubbed shoulders with elders in comical straw hats. Seated on the podium between the poet, Nancy Morejon (whom I had met on several occasions in Guadeloupe, Martinique as well as the US), and Marco Alexander (a translator from the university), I was soon overcome with a feeling that was hard to explain. Different from what I had experienced in Japan several years earlier. The purpose of literature is not only to draw people from very different cultures closer together, to have them unite in close intimacy, but also to build bridges of love between individuals. Gabriel García Márquez, who said, 'I write to be loved', would have been overjoyed. Suddenly I was transformed: I became the mother, daughter and sister of everyone around me. I was caught up in a flow of warmth which streamed from the hearts and minds of the audience.

My book *I, Tituba* had been translated into Cuban Spanish for a publication that was priced so that everyone could buy it. I signed so many copies that I came over dizzy and, amid general concern, had to go outside into the garden and breathe in some fresh air. The sun had set with that suddenness so special to our islands. Night had fallen. A cool breeze blew in from the sea which was singing softly a few metres distant on the other side of the Malecon. I was filled with a happiness I had never felt before.

Fabienne Viala, a young university professor from Paris V, specially invited to introduce *Tituba* to these budding readers, came over to me. 'We're having dinner at friends' tonight,' she announced. 'You should avoid eating out. Either the restaurants are very bad or they're outrageously expensive and just as bad. Casa de Las Americas is so hard up it can only afford one meal, tomorrow evening I think at the Hotel Nacional, Havana's biggest hotel.'

Havana was badly lit and somewhat disconcerting as soon as night fell. The meagre light from its lampposts never managed to quite dispel the darkness. The many passers-by walking through the streets took on strange shadowy shapes. The doorways to the houses looked like dark holes.

Fabienne's friends lived on the edge of the old town. 'They are planning to take you there for a visit,' she said. 'It's very lovely, a real jewel. The municipality has not skimped on expense and has restored over a hundred historic buildings.'

We had to climb up a very dark, steep stairway to the third floor since there was no lift in that old edifice. Two young couples, around thirty, and their children were waiting for us. The two women were nurses at the same hospital, the two men government employees. Their flat was spacious though somewhat sparsely furnished. Unfortunately, they spoke practically no French and even less English. They were visibly intimidated by our presence but brimming with consideration and warmth. We began by drinking to our health with mojitos (which in my opinion cannot hold a candle to our rum punches, be they with fruit or lime and sugar). We were then served an extremely simple meal of roast pork, fried plantains, rice and black beans. It was very savoury and we did it credit.

'You've no idea,' Fabienne whispered during the coconut-flan dessert which reminded me of Adélia, 'how much trouble they went through to invite you. Their resources are limited. They are only allowed access to the stores where you pay in Cuban pesos and which stock the mere basics.'

I was only too familiar with such a system: state-sponsored stores where you pay in a devalued currency and stores where the better-off pay in foreign currency. My head was buzzing with questions which out of discretion I dared not ask. What did our hosts think of the Revolution? We were, of course, well aware of its remarkable achievements in the fields of education and health. Its teachers and physicians were used to aiding developing countries throughout the world. But what was it like in daily life? To dress, drink, eat, invite friends, raise children and spoil them?

We took our leave shortly before midnight. It was impossible to find a taxi, so Richard and I returned to the hotel on foot along the Malecon. Fabienne was by no means reassured. She said the place was dangerous and known for its muggings. I turned a deaf ear since I hadn't breathed in the smell of the sea for a long time nor felt its caress on my face. We did not have any unpleasant encounters except for some dogs copulating silently in the dark. The hotel lift was again out of order; we had to squeeze in with several other guests into a service lift which fortunately was working.

The following day we were dragged out of bed at eight in the morning. A reader was waiting for us on the hotel terrace where a swarm of young girls had already begun their ploys around the tourists. She apologized: she had not been able to come to Casa de Las Americas the day before but wanted absolutely for her book to be signed. She was a mulatto woman with almost white skin, lovely under her thick tangle of salt-and-pepper hair, wearing a striped cotton dress cut low at the shoulders. Her authoritarian, somewhat sharp manner, betrayed her origins. She spoke perfect French and English. She introduced herself as Eugénia Reynolds. Did her name suggest her husband was American?

She handed me a small painting wrapped in paper strips like a mummy. 'I've brought you this,' she said. 'I did it myself. I'm a painter and a poet in my spare time. I wanted my painting to be on the cover of *Tituba* but it was too expensive for Casa de Las Americas, so they refused.'

I undid the paper strips one by one and stopped short. The painting was strangely beautiful—a black woman in a red corset, crouching in the middle of a courtyard. Holding a toad whose long claws twined around her fingers. Looking straight ahead with her enormous eyes. Her hair was tousled. In such circumstances, any words of thanks always seem artificial and conventional. Yet I did my best.

We invited her to join us for breakfast but she shook her head contemptuously. 'If it weren't for you,' she explained, 'I would never set foot in such a place. These hotels are awful.'

Nevertheless she followed us into the dining room and sat down at our table, sweeping the surroundings with the same critical and contemptuous look, and grudgingly responded to friendly greetings from the Venezuelan footballers.

'It's a pity you're not staying longer. I would have taken you to my house by the sea. We would have dined on fruit and fresh fish. You would not have caught dysentery by staying here.'

It was obvious I would have no trouble getting her opinion on the Revolution. But it wasn't the one I wanted to hear. I wanted a balanced and objective opinion. Balanced and objective? Does it exist? Had I myself given a balanced and objective opinion of Guinea in *Heremakhonon*? Points of view are always subjective.

'I've heard a lot about you,' she continued. 'My daughter teaches in Winnipeg with a Guadeloupean girl who was at school with you. My son lives in Canada. He's a doctor in Montreal. I'm all alone here. My husband was Canadian. When we divorced, I left the children with him. It was for the better. Now I only see them once or twice a year. As a rule on my birthday. As you know, we are unable to travel outside the country.'

There was a silence, then she resumed in her slightly theatrical voice. 'I know what you're thinking. I could have left like the others, like so many others. Our Cuban exiles have kidnapped Florida from the Americans who fear us, yet try to win us over. Unfortunately, I love my country. I couldn't live or paint anywhere else. It's fundamental to me. I admire you for being able to continue writing despite abandoning Guadeloupe.'

'I haven't abandoned Guadeloupe,' I protested. 'I always spend Christmas and the summer holidays there.'

'Three months a year,' she scoffed. 'Is that enough for you?'

Cut to the quick, I endeavoured to justify myself. 'A country is not just a physical space, a geographical reality. It is above all a series of sensations, impressions and a frame of mind, an interior landscape deep inside yourself.'

At that moment, two representatives from Casa de Las Americas made their way towards us, to fetch us for that highly popular visit of the old town. I was obliged to say goodbye to Eugénia whereas I would have preferred to continue our conversation which was verging on the essential. Exile? I was not a believer, I who had been treated like an outsider when I was among my own people. I will say it again and would have liked to have convinced Eugénia: You carry your country with you and re-imagine it to your heart's content.

Our guides were very enthusiastic. One of them insisted on taking us to see an important monument, El Templete, that pays homage to the spot where the town was founded in 1519. All morning, amid a throng of tourists from the world over, we wandered through the narrow winding streets, diving with them under the arcades, trudging through vast rooms in historic mansions, crossing small plazas, refreshing ourselves with the water from the fountains and taking photos of just about everything. For lunch, we went with the flow and ate at the Bodeguita del Medio, steps from the cathedral of San Cristobal and El Patio cutting through Empedrado street. This seemingly modest bar cum restaurant has been made famous by Ernest Hemingway, and serves excellent mojitos. As for the lunch of roast pork, fried plantains, rice and black beans—it was reminiscent of the dinner at Fabienne's friends the day before but much less tasty.

It was not difficult to guess that Havana was no longer a gourmet's paradise. Whenever he was in Paris, René Depestre would take me to the Celtique, a small bar opposite the Présence Africaine book-store. He would tell me about Cuba where he still lived. He would describe the sumptuous days when they used to spit roast a whole sheep stuffed with aromatic herbs and slices of sugarcane, cook guinea fowl with coarse salt, pineapples stuffed with meat and fish cooked in foil. Evidently, those days were over. The age of survival had taken over with all its restrictions. René also talked about the virulent racism in Cuba. 'Previously,' he told me, 'a rope sep-arated the theatres and dance halls in two, so that the blacks wouldn't come and bother the whites and the Mulattos. It was Fidel who changed all that.'

When I met the Cuban, Carlos Moore, I heard another story. If you were to go by what he said, Fidel had done nothing and racism remained the scourge of Cuba. I must confess that all around me everyone was so kind that I had no intention of hunt-ing down racism to see whether it still existed.

I know, I know, in many respects I didn't make the most out of my stay in Cuba. I didn't make time to admire the old town, such a rare and precious architectural ensemble in our Caribbean islands where everything seems to boil down to plunder and barter. During the official dinner of about twenty set-tings that Casa de Las Americas organized in my hon-our at the Hotel Nacional, I did not pay enough attention to the numerous photos of Clark Gable, Errol Flynn, Gary Cooper and Rita Hayworth, that clique of Hollywood stars who rushed to the island when it was, as Fanon said, the bordello of the West.

I didn't take enough time to track down Hemingway whose books I have read. I didn't bother to visit the house he owned on the outskirts of Havana which is now a museum. I was only interested in the anonymous individuals who crossed my path. I did not try to decipher whether the Revolution had really brought them happiness. I spent long hours with them at Casa de Las Americas, signing copies of *Tituba* and making limited conversation because of the language barrier. I wanted to keep intact for ever the feelings of fraternity they inspired me with.

Shortly before the end of our stay, the Siyaj theatre troupe arrived from Guadeloupe to perform my play *Like Two Brothers*. I had written it for Gilbert Laumord whom I have known for years. In 1989, he played the role of Zephyr, the narrator, in my play commissioned by Félix Proto, president of the Regional Council of Guadeloupe, to commemorate the bicentenary of the French Revolution. Gilbert was a regular visitor to Cuba. He had often worked with the director Eugenio Hernández Espinosa, analysing the relationship between our traditional tales and modern theatre, endeavouring to identify the continuum between the past and the present. Gilbert had invited Eugenio to Guadeloupe on several occasions as well as performed in Cuba. Consequently, although the text of *Like Two Brothers* was in French, the Cubans came in great numbers to both shows, laughing and applauding as if they understood every word.

On the last evening, the skies opened and the streets were flooded from the downpour. The event was exceptional since the weather had remained perfect all week long. According to the popular saying, it meant that I would be sorry to leave. And it was true—I was sorry to have to leave, to say goodbye to all those friends and the island of Cuba.

In the course of a week, it seemed I was back in the womb and safe from everything.

The Land of Milk and Honey

My visit to Israel, however, was dominated by debate, even confusion and difficulties. My press attaché at Mercure de France publishers told me that a certain writer from Martinique had also been invited to Israel but refused the invitation since he had no intention of supporting the politics of the current government. Did I want to do the same? I was in a quandary. After thinking it over, I decided to go ahead. To my knowledge, it was not an official invitation—it was from the French cultural services and not the Israeli government who had certainly never heard of me. It meant no more than a harmless literary discussion with readers, a moment of diversion that had nothing to do with politics.

My friend Louise Yellin begged me not to go, somewhat for the same reasons as the writer from Martinique. 'It'll be risky. They'll ask you for your opinion on everything, even the withdrawal of Israel from the Occupied Territories.'

'I'd be very surprised if they did,' I replied, shrugging. 'How could anyone take seriously the opinion of an unknown writer on such a major subject that is setting the whole world at odds?'

Maryse Condé

My friend Ronnie Scharfman, on the other hand, begged me not to give up my visit, and told me of numerous Jewish associations in Tel Aviv who were engaged in the Palestinian cause. I had trouble convincing her that I would certainly not have enough time in the space of a week to contact them. I had other much more pressing concerns. My son, recently returned from Africa and embarked upon a relatively successful career as a writer, had been diagnosed HIV positive the previous year and was one of the first patients to experiment triple-combination therapy. He spent his time going in and out of hospital. We never knew how long he would stay in his apartment on the Place des Abbesses. It was agonizing. Right up to the day before our departure, we still didn't know whether we could leave.

If the Cuban immigration officers seemed to us finicky and inquisitive, what could we say about the Israeli? Ignoring Richard, protected perhaps by his colour and British passport, they questioned me unrelentingly. For almost an hour, three men with inscrutable faces interrogated me. I had to swear I had no affiliation with the countries of North Africa and that I had never been a Communist, a ridiculous assumption since I was working and living in the States. At one point I felt like turning my back on those hostile officials who were presenting me with such an inhospitable image of their country. The plane was full of Orthodox Jews, the ones I had seen in Brooklyn, their hair curling down to their shoulders under their dark felt hats, followed by a trail of children and stout wives in wigs. I'm fond of children, I'm always delighted by their spontaneity and curiosity. I soon found myself playing with a group of girls one of whom fell asleep in my arms.

We arrived very late in Tel Aviv. As soon as we drove into town, I was struck by the atmosphere. Groups of boys and girls gaily roamed the brilliantly lit streets on foot or on motorbikes. Music was being performed in the city squares. Seated on benches, old people were singing and keeping time. I couldn't believe my eyes. I thought the Israelis would be gloomy and sombre, obsessed with their disastrous confrontation with the Palestinians. Apparently, they were nothing of the sort.

We checked in to our hotel and went for a drink. Two young men sat down familiarly at our table. 'What brings you to Israel?' they asked.

They confessed they had never heard of me but politely promised to read one of my books if they could find a copy. But they knew about Guadeloupe and Martinique—they had worked on board the *Costa Serena*, a cruise ship which docked in several ports in the Caribbean. They had stayed in Saint Barthélemy and worked as waiters in a hotel.

'Enjoy your stay in Israel,' they said as they took their leave.

I had also been asked to present another book which, unlike *I, Tituba*, had not been translated into Hebrew. It was a children's book called *At the Bend of the Joliba*, for which I had written the text and my

Italian friend, Letizia Galli, had done the illustrations. We had both gone to Guadeloupe to promote the book. The schoolchildren there, little conversant with the surrealists' pictorial distortions, had bombarded Letizia with questions: 'Why did you give your characters three eyes?' 'Why did you give them two noses?'

The elementary school where I had been invited was in Jaffa, on the outskirts of Tel Aviv. Since the distances in Israel are very short, we had time to tour Tel Aviv. The city was not lacking in charm. A radiant sun beamed down on the rows of luxury buildings along the seafront. Tanned young people filled the tennis courts or sunbathed on the golden beaches. All of which was in strong contrast to the images I had of deeply religious ascetics praying in front of the Wailing Wall or solemn rabbis with flowing beards.

At the school in Jaffa, a class of ten-year-olds was waiting for me: twenty adorable schoolchildren as good as gold under mops of black, curly hair. But soon I realized that this encounter would be very different from the one in Guadeloupe—these children were not at all interested in *At the Bend of the Joliba*, although they had studied it with their teacher. All they were interested in was me.

'Are there Jews in Guadeloupe?' one of them asked.

I searched my brain. I believe a synagogue had recently opened at Bas-du-Fort.

'What do they think about us where you live?' asked another. While I was thinking of an answer, a third said: 'They don't like us there either, do they?'

Whereas I wasn't in the least prepared for it, these children brutally catapulted me to the very heart of the Israeli problem. I mustered all my resources of tact and diplomacy and tried to moderate my answers. And I recalled Louise's warning. She was right. If the children's questions possessed such intensity, what would the grown-ups' be like whom I was to meet late afternoon? I spent some of the most difficult hours of my life in that class and emerged quaking at the knees. Then, with the teaching staff, we had an excellent lunch close by: diced, grilled liver and eggplant puree. But I was beginning to understand that this visit to Israel would not boil down to discovering savoury recipes.

Around four in the afternoon, a limousine from the French cultural services drove us the 60 kilometres to Jerusalem where I was a guest at the prestigious writer's residence of Mishkenot Sha'Ananim. The road was lined with a never-ending succession of orchards loaded with fruit. It was difficult to imagine that this had once been a desert, an expanse of stones and brambles. The incredible ingenuity of the Israelis had achieved a miracle. I couldn't help thinking too of my mother who was so pious, so devout. How she would have loved to be in my shoes, to be at the very cradle of Christianity; to visit the Holy Places; kneel at Golgotha and meditate at

Christ's tomb. What for me was merely a banal tourist visit for her would have been a deep and inestimable pilgrimage.

The Mishkenot Sha'Ananim writer's residence was housed in a magnificent palace surrounded by a garden filled with all sorts of fruit trees. Unfortunately, we were the only guests, so there were just the two of us to indulge in all that sumptuousness and beauty.

On our arrival, I was surprised to find the auditorium at the French Cultural Centre absolutely full. I wondered who these men and women were, who had given up their daily routine to listen to an unknown writer whom they probably had never read. I bravely turned to speak, and realized that the situation wasn't going to be as easy as in Tokyo or Cuba. I had always objected to a certain reading of *I, Tituba*. That's why I didn't care too much for the preface by Angela Davis who had transformed the book's humour and derision into a serious, political engagement. Here I could sense that it would not be a question of interpreting a novel but of focusing on me: me, the writer, the author, Maryse Condé. The one Roland Barthes declared dead. The writer who was never visible in the lecture rooms where literature was studied. Suddenly, I came back to life. I retrieved my work. Before following where I intended to take them, the audience insisted I define myself in relation to them, that I define myself politically. They would not make one move in my direction until I clearly stated what I thought of them.

My opinion on the Israel–Palestine conflict is, I confess, summary, perhaps even simplistic. To deny the right of Israel to exist has never crossed my mind, and I'm probably eluding the fundamental problem. My friends Louise and Ronnie have described to me in stark unsentimental terms the suffering and persecution of their parents, the reasons for their exile in the land of America and their painstaking efforts to integrate. I even dreamt of introducing some of their memories in one of my novels. I have to admit that seeing the United States constantly fly to the assistance of Israel fills me with a feeling of injustice. I ended up believing that the conflict between Israel and Palestine was a new version of David versus Goliath, minus the happy end obviously. I pitied the Palestinians and considered them the victims. That is what I endeavoured to explain in all humility but firmly for over two hours to a polite but overexcited audience. While they slowly made their way out, chattering in small groups, a young woman came over to me accompanied by a bald-headed, somewhat pudgy man.

'You handled that quite well,' she said. 'Don't be surprised if they can't talk about anything else here except Palestine.'

'I'm worn out,' I said with a sigh. She took me by the arm. 'A good rum punch will help you recover. Can we invite you two for dinner?'

She was from Martinique. Her name was Vincente and her husband was Nathan. They had lived for twelve years in Jerusalem, Nathan's birth-place.

Outside, the din and sights of the street were extraordinary. In a small square, a group was beating drums in the middle of a circle of frenzied dancers. Crowds of young people roamed around, chatting and laughing. But what struck me the most was the sight of guards, armed to the teeth, stationed in front of the entrances to the bars and restaurants.

'What are they afraid of?' I murmured aghast.

'We're in Jerusalem,' Vincente and Nathan said in unison, as if that was sufficient explanation.

Since they lived close to the French Cultural Centre, we walked to their place, an elegant flat furnished with white sofas strewn with mauve-coloured cushions. From their balcony you faced the huge wall built by the Israelis in order to contain the freedom of movement by the Palestinians. It was horrible. I took comfort nevertheless in the meal that followed: fish balls in a creamy saffron sauce accompanied by caramelized turnips.

'It's Sephardic cooking,' Vincente explained, proud and happy that I had done justice to her meal, 'since my husband's family is from Morocco. Israeli cuisine is extraordinary, it is so varied. It includes dishes from all the people who came to settle in the country.'

Thereupon she launched into a detailed description of the dishes her mother-in-law lovingly prepared. 'If you like I can take you to buy some recipe books.'

We were soon submerged by the eagerness and kindness of everyone around us, provided there was no mention of the relationship with the Palestinians. Complete strangers went out of their way to help us take advantage of the surrounding sights. A couple drove us to Jericho in the Occupied Territories, one of the oldest cities in the region; another took us to dinner at the American Colony Hotel where we sat down to an unforgettable feast. That magnificent hotel boasted among its guests personalities as varied as Lawrence of Arabia, Tony Blair and Philip Roth. We travelled with a group to a resort on the banks of the Dead Sea, crowded with swimmers where young women wore daring two-piece swimsuits. The water was flat and dark, just right for drowning, I thought. I refused to go in for a swim, since water gives me panic attacks, a fear dating back to my childhood. My parents' change-of-air house was situated not far from the beach at Viard, not at all a lovely beach, nothing by comparison to those which Grande Terre and the Leeward coast boasted of. You had to cross a thicket of bushes as dense as a mangrove in order to get to the beach of black, muddy sand on which a dismal sea untiringly spewed up bunches of seaweed. But it wasn't the ugliness of the place that oppressed me. It was because Adélia had told me a story (true or false?) which kept running through my head: a white planter in the neighbourhood had raped Amélie, one of his slaves. It was common practice, Adélia explained serenely, which horrified me. As a rule slaves who were raped never breathed a word; and nine months later, gave birth to a baby mulatto. That was not the case with Amélie who preferred to drown herself at Viard. Her body drifted in the water for days, seaweed clinging to her pubis, until some sailors fished her out.

I gathered strength during the day to prepare myself for the evenings which always proved difficult. For Vincente's sake, I agreed to a book-signing in a bookstore owned by one of her friends. Customers came in great numbers but I didn't sell a single copy. All they could talk about was the recent terrorist attack in East Jerusalem. The attackers, three young Palestinians, had been shot dead. A woman addressed me sharply but calmly with a deep sense of sorrow: 'You see: they want to destroy us, eliminate us! And yet you go on defending them.'

Me? I was defending nobody. I had not been sufficiently briefed.

Everything in Haifa got off to an auspicious start. Our hotel overhung the sea, a sumptuous blue carpet that unrolled as far as the horizon. Richard and I were charmed by this town where Jews and Arabs lived side by side in apparent harmony. We lunched on a couscous in a delightful restaurant two steps from an enormous Bahá'í temple.

There was a crowd at the cultural centre. For an hour we even managed to talk about literature and

Tituba. At question time, unfortunately, a young man stood up and questioned me on the iniquitous treatment of the Falasha Jews and the many African immigrants. What did I have to say on the question? Immediately, some people took issue with him. The discussion grew bitter. Everyone began to scream and shout. Fearing for our safety, the two organizers preferred to put an end to the meeting and gave the order to evacuate the room. On the pavement outside, a man came over to me: 'That's how it is here. The women are against the men, the young against the old. Those who come from Europe despise those who come from Africa and so on.'

How creditworthy were his words? I was incapable of judging.

On the way back to the hotel, Richard and I had a dreadful fright. A group of half a dozen young men began to follow us, stopping whenever they drew too close. It looked as though they were Arabs but we couldn't be sure, the irony being that Jews and Arabs often look alike. Safely back in our hotel room, we ran to the window. They were still there, sitting on a bench in the small square opposite the hotel. Some were smoking. Others were talking and gesticulating. Who were they? Innocent passers-by? Then why had they followed us? Were they from the audience at the cultural centre who wanted to continue the discussion? When we looked out of the window around midnight, they were gone. We never got to know what they wanted.

We left for Tel Aviv the following morning. The discussion in the afternoon at the cultural centre lasted almost four hours. Nobody attacked me verbally, nobody was discourteous. Yet the barrage of questions had nothing to do with literature. I was not prepared for it, and it exhausted me. I got the impression of being easy prey, thrown to wild beasts which at any moment could turn ferocious. Even if nobody dreamt of devouring me, I couldn't help trembling with fright.

I could have kept unpleasant memories of my stay in Israel. But this was not the case. The delicious food I tasted during both trendy invitations as well as in small cafes had a lot to do with it. At the American Colony Hotel, for example, the menu was filled with attractive dishes: hummus, bean puree, eggplant confit, braised mutton and chicken with lemons and small onions. Yet I was glad to be back in New York: this hectic, pulsating rush of a city seemed in contrast a haven of peace. It was because, once again, I was happily anonymous, and nobody wanted to make me be what I wasn't.

My life returned to being calm and intellectual. In my seminar, my students discussed in earnest *In Praise of Creoleness* . They assailed me with questions: 'Why have you never written in Creole?' 'Have you never been tempted to do so?' 'Do you think that one day you'll write in Creole?' asked a third.

It was in answer to all these interrogations that I began to think about my relationship with the two languages. I ended up concocting the phrase I have so often repeated: 'I don't write in French, I write in Maryse Condé.' Yet I subtly shifted the focus of my classes. I realized that literature cannot entirely be divorced from politics. Whether it likes it or not, in spite of its silences, every work is politically committed. Angela Davis was right. *I, Tituba* was not only my creation, a medium for anachronism, a pretext for derision—it was also a testimony to the condition of black women in seventeenth-century America.

Back from my travels, I usually invited our friends to sample a dish whose recipe I had recently discovered. On our return from Israel, I cooked a series of dishes of various origins which I had seen prepared. The high point of the meal was lamb with lemon and garlic, a Sephardic dish I had tasted at Vincente's.

The following year started out sad and sorrowful. I couldn't get over the death of my son and my depression pulled me down to rock bottom. Incapable of writing, I couldn't help turning over and over again in my head the turbulent years we had spent together, the constant quarrels, the too-short reconciliations, until the end when we finally came to terms with each other. Once again he was the little boy he used to be, shy, gentle and fond of his mother. I, however, influenced by the clichés of the time, found him too effeminate and constantly rejected him. I sent him off to holiday camps and courses where you learnt to run, swim and box, things he loathed but tried to do his best in order to satisfy me. God, I have so much to blame myself for.

I didn't have the strength to travel but Richard forced me to accept conference invitations from neighbouring universities. So I caught the train for Boston at Penn Station. I like American trains which take days to cover distances that the French high-speed trains cover in hours. I like Boston too, a cold, aristocratic city with elegant brick houses. Part of my novel *Desirada* takes place there when Marie-Noëlle, after so many setbacks and false starts, becomes a professor of literature.

It was autumn. The treetops were turning red, orange and yellow; you felt you were walking through the sumptuous, secret sets of an opera. Jutta M'Bahya, who had invited me, was married to a Cameroonian political refugee. Her mother-in-law regularly mailed her food parcels. We had a surprising dinner of cassava sticks called *miondo* and an excellent brown pâté which I had never tasted before. When I asked for the ingredients, I was told it was composed of insects, a mixture of red ants and a variety of caterpillars. I still don't know how my stomach supported such a revelation.

I also accepted an invitation by Awa Soumaoro, a young Muslim professor who taught at the great Catholic University of Notre Dame. I arrived fairly early in order to attend mass and sat down in the chapel filled with devoutly praying students. I let myself go with the flow to the altar where I took communion, something I hadn't done in years. Taking communion without having confessed? Perhaps I had committed a mortal sin. My childhood convictions reasserted themselves and I awaited punishment for this act of sacrilege. But, as usual, God did not manifest Himself.

In the evening, the Colombian head of the department organized a dinner of thick corn soup, potatoes, chicken and pork. It was a special dish from her country called Aijaco santafereno. I made the mistake of expressing an interest, and she dragged me into her office and typed out on her computer for almost an hour the best recipes from Colombia.

At Montclair in New Jersey, another head of department, a Chilean this time, served up a stew of fish heads whose bones almost asphyxiated me.

Despite these often comical events, I dragged myself along in a sluggish state. I would spend hours on a bench in Riverside Park without a glance at either the children muffled up to their necks, the joggers or the dog-walkers. I blamed myself again and again for not having understood my son.

At his wit's end, Richard convinced me to accept an invitation in May to the Calabash Festival in Jamaica. The sun, the sea and talking with other writers might give me a change of mind. We had already visited Jamaica and knew Professor Michael Dash who was teaching there at the time. The country had a lot of appeal. I had borrowed the Waterloo Guest House in Black River and turned it into a love nest for Thécla, the heroine of my novel *Tree of Life*. We had travelled the length and breadth of Maroon country which was said to be so violent. We had gone down to the bottom of a valley to pay homage on the supposed tomb of Nanny of the Maroons who had routed the English troops in the eighteenth century. In a five-star hotel in Ocho Rios, we had dined on a typically English meal of leg of lamb, mint sauce and boiled vegetables. I have a memory of the immaculate beach at Negril, deserted except for the Rasta men and their blonde American women, stretching out as far as the eye could see.

We were unprepared, therefore, for the hordes of American tourists in Montego Bay: men and women, black and white, some decidedly overweight, dressed identically in ungainly shorts and flowery shirts.

Fortunately, we were able to escape fairly quickly since the Calabash Festival was three hours away by road, near Black River. The beauty of Jamaica is well known. All kinds of harmonious landscapes rolled by to the left and right of the car: neat, rounded hills covered with lush vegetation, razor sharp cliffs as well as stretches of semi desert.

We arrived at Black River as night fell. Our hotel, Jake's Place, was situated a few miles further, in the village of Treasure Beach. It was a charming place composed of cottages arranged over a large garden and a sunken pool. It overlooked a vast sea whose waves rippled as far as the horizon. Though the dinner that followed did not prove as good as the setting. Fortunately, the sounds of a reggae group quickly dissipated our disappointment. I was surprised by the crowds who pushed in to find a place to sit, even on the ground and along the garden paths.

I soon discovered that the Calabash Festival had a personality all its own, which explained its popular success. It had become an institution and a yearly event. The radio and newspapers covered the entire programme. The organizers made a point of inviting well-known writers; that year there was Michael Ondaatje, Caryl Phillips, Kwame Dawes, Colin Channer and a quartet of African American female poets. But they were incidental, compared to the Festival's somewhat unorthodox regulations:

One, every individual has a story of his own to tell.

Two, there are no rules to storytelling and everyone is free to express themselves as they please.

Three, education is not the only criterion to explain creativity. An individual said to be 'uneducated' can have a wealth of resources.

Four, publishing imprisons the word. There is no need to be published; we must safeguard the spontaneity of orality.

Five, women are just as creative as men.

I was by no means convinced by these rules. For me, literature is a tough vocation which can only be acquired at the cost of a wider knowledge of the world. It involves an extensive culture.

Below the hotel's garden stood two huge tents: one housed the cafeteria where you could eat at any hour; and the other, rows of chairs and a small platform with a mike. Open-mike sessions were organized daily. Those who wanted to tell their story in public first registered their name, then took as long as they liked, even twice a day if they so wanted. The open-mike sessions attracted a lot of people. They came from as far away as Kingston, the capital, and Port Antonio.

Richard and I went to these sessions. To tell the truth, I disliked them, was even bored by them. What claimed to pass for spontaneity seemed to me a lack of hard work. Most of the narratives were unoriginal and repetitive. The women complained time and time again of the men's machismo, of their children's possessiveness and the little time left to write. As for the men: they lamented the harshness and indifference of a society too preoccupied with material success.

Nowhere could I detect a particular talent. Their whining seemed extremely trivial. I felt out of place during the endless debates that inflamed the spectators. I tried to make contact with a few women, but they greeted me lukewarmly. I suppose my status as a university professor put them off. I was, whether or not I liked it, the tedious sermonizer, the schoolmistress.

Even so, I managed to get to know a certain Edna. In a long prose poem, she had described her feelings on the death of her daughter. Her text made a deep impact on me. It echoed my own remorse. Edna's character was not exactly agreeable. She refused the slightest criticism and considered her work to be perfect. Her profound feeling of superiority was stimulated by an enthusiastic review in the local press. She even allowed herself the luxury of refusing publication with Jamaica's sole publishing house. I accepted to be treated like a novice, like a beginner, since literature is also a school of humility. Edna had to leave the festival before the end and return to her native Port Antonio where she was the guest of honour at a cultural evening.

The festival food was greasy and heavy—curried goat and jerk pork, thick slices of smoked pork, consistently garnished with rice. As a consequence, we had got into the habit of eating out at Treasure Beach, a somewhat pretty fishermen's village. The Captain Nemo restaurant, which was advantageously situated on the water, had become our refuge. There at least the fish was fresh.

One lunch time we met Kwame Dawes and one of the African American poets, Laura Adamson. Despite her extreme discretion, she attended the open-mike sessions without ever asking a question. I knew she was professor of philosophy at Yale. Her poems were published in *Sulfur*, a highly esteemed journal in the States.

We had barely sat down at the same table than Laura exclaimed, taking me as witness: 'Isn't this festival wonderful? I'm going to ask some of the women for permission to include their stories in an ode I'm working on.'

I took the liberty of making a few modest objections. Couldn't we recommend that these writers, even if they claimed to be different, do more work on their texts? Emotion is not sufficient as a medium. You need also to research the choice of words and metaphors.

'You're elitist,' Laura laughed.

Was that true? I was about to defend myself when Laura resumed. 'Come to my room tomorrow afternoon to meet some of these writers. It'll be more private.'

Somewhat stung, I didn't follow up on Laura's invitation. Overcoming my fears of the water, I preferred to opt for a boat trip organized by the festival. Little did I realize what lay in store. The festival-goers had to pile into a number of small boats and sail up the dark, murky waters of the Black River as it wound between steep banks and passed creeks where half-naked men brought their cattle to drink. We stopped at Port Grove, a tavern wide open to the sun, belonging to a couple of white Jamaicans with brick-red cheeks. The meal was generous. Besides the inevitable jerk pork, which could be taken for the national dish, Lucy and Terrence served up ackees and salt fish, ackees being a kind of fruit which I am incapable of describing. Everyone knew the couple and they knew everyone, and there were good-natured slaps on the back everywhere.

Around three in the afternoon, we sailed back down the Black River to its mouth. There we were taken out far from the seashore. Emerging out of the waves, a metal staircase led up to a rudimentary platform housing a bar. The effect was mind-boggling since the entire edifice swayed left and right, drifting with the underwater currents. It felt as though at any moment we would all sink beneath the waves. While the others dashed to get their rum punches, I remained gripping my table.

'What are you afraid of?' Kwame Dawes scoffed. 'We're all expert swimmers. If you fall in, we'll come and fish you out, it's as simple as that.'

This trip to Jamaica did not result in a miraculous cure. Nevertheless, I was able to take up my life again. The past was past and I could do nothing about it. I went back to my office and began writing again: the novel that went on to become *The Last of the African Kings*. On rereading it, I realized it was echoing the concerns addressed by the Calabash Festival. When the character of Djéré endeavours to write down the traditional tales told to him by his grandfather while he was a little boy, he expresses my thoughts on the relationship between oral and written literature. Jean-Jacques Rousseau, who we know hated books, declares the superiority of oral literature over the written word. In substance, he goes as far as comparing the latter to a corpse in which we would have trouble seeking the beauty of the living person. I believe such claims to be exaggerated. Oral and written literature are closely linked, each attempting to impose its own stamp.

As for me, I need music to write and I am keenly interested in all types of music. Which boils down to saying that I am not too far from oral literature.

My contacts with Laura Adamson stopped when we left Jamaica. Although Yale is not too far from Columbia, we made no attempt to see each other again. About a year after our meeting, she sent me

a book called *Hubbub*. It involved a long penetra-
ting and nostalgic poem which was not lacking in
charm. I thought I recognized Edna's story. Yet it
had been so purged, so reworked and transformed
that I wasn't sure. I sent Laura a set of conventional,
meaningless congratulations. It was only years later
that I was to see her again in rather unexpected
circumstances.

N'KOSI SIKELEL 'IAFRIKA

I must confess I have never been a fervent militant in
the fight against apartheid, even though I obviously
believe the system to be iniquitous. In the universities
where I taught, I of course took part in all the
marches and demonstrations. I signed petitions and
repeated the slogan 'disinvest' which the students
hurled at administrations bent on trading with the
hateful country. But my heart wasn't in it. I believed
South Africa's problem, which got so much media
coverage and that the whole world seemed set on
condemning and trying to resolve, masked a blatant
indifference regarding offences committed against
other lesser-known peoples. Obviously when Nelson
Mandela was released from prison on 11 February
1990, I was touched by the magic of the couple he
formed with his wife Winnie: both so handsome, so
noble. Obviously, I was affected by their separation
and lamented their divorce. I never stopped admiring
Winnie and stubbornly refused to believe in the
charges against her. In my eyes, she embodied a kind
of revolutionary violence that confounded the com-
promises demanded by the exercise of power.

As a fervent disciple of Frantz Fanon, I had difficulty accepting the creation of the Truth and Reconciliation Commission. Hadn't my intellectual guide asserted that, in order to be reborn, man must be baptized with the blood of his torturer? This notion of reconciliation was no doubt the brainchild of Desmond Tutu. Men of the cloth should never mess with politics. Here was blatant proof. South Africa remained for me a distant, somewhat mythical land. You can imagine my stupefaction, then elation, when I received not one but two invitations.

The first was from Time of the Writer Festival organized every year in Durban; and the second from Françoise Verges who begged me to take part in a conference on black aesthetics organized by the French cultural services in Cape Town. The problem was that the two events were over a month apart. Richard and I launched into a series of desperate calculations to see whether we could stay all that time in a country where we knew absolutely no one. We required hotel accommodation, restaurant meals and a car if we wanted to travel around as we pleased. Without managing to work out a budget and placing ourselves in the grace of God, we resolutely boarded the flight from Atlanta to Durban via Johannesburg.

I cannot describe how disappointed I was from the very first day. Whereas the Calabash Festival had a personality all its own, with wide media coverage and crowds of spectators, Time of the Writer was a humdrum routine of lectures and round tables in half-empty rooms. Thanks to money from their sponsors, the organizers had managed to invite a group of prestigious writers, including Sylvie Germain and Nancy Huston from France; Margaret Drabble and Joanna Trollope from the UK; and Ahmadou Kourouma from the Ivory Coast. But the writers apparently had nothing to say and were not the least interested in being where they were. Joanna Trollope had no scruples leaving on a solo tour of the country's bookstores; a few days later, Nancy Huston disappeared as well to meet Coetzee and Breyten Breytenbach in Cape Town. Attending the conference soon became a chore. But what else was there to do?

The Nightingale Hotel was situated on a long stretch of beach facing the flat, faded blue of the Indian Ocean, spiked with nets against marauding sharks. It was enough to discourage any thought of swimming. Only a few were bold enough to venture out a few feet from the shore. Around ten in the morning, a bus came to pick us up and took us reluctantly to the cultural centre. We drove through the suburbs of Durban, a conglomeration of identical apartment blocks all with flower-bedecked balconies. The town centre was just as drab: rectilinear streets crisscrossed at right angles, perfectly pruned trees planted at equal distance along the pavements and grass-covered squares with fencing to keep out animals.

The town housed an apartheid museum. Much to the disappointment of visitors, all it had to offer were poor-quality monochrome photos of a time gone by. Durban's only charm was its large choice of Indian restaurants because of the ethnic origin of its inhabitants. We became regulars at the Oriental Palace which, despite its pretentious name, was merely a small cafe.

The Indians in Durban were not at all like those I met in India. On the contrary, they were bursting with kindness. Most of them had never heard of Guadeloupe so I had to deliver a short geography and sociology lesson to inform them about the large Indian population in the French Antilles.

'You should go to Pietermaritzburg,' Srinivas, one of the waiters told us. 'That's where a white man threw the young lawyer Mohandas Gandhi off the train because he was enraged that an Indian was travelling First Class. That's when the nonviolence movement was born.'

For reasons I never understood, or perhaps because I was from Guadeloupe, out of all the writers I was the one chosen to converse with a class at a Muslim college whose name I have forgotten. I was welcomed in a grand hall where portraits of a dozen moustachioed men took pride of place: probably Muslim VIPs whom I had never heard of. About thirty Indian teenagers elegantly dressed in yellow-and-green uniforms were waiting for me under the supervision of a dozen, ferocious-faced teachers acting as bodyguards. They immediately addressed a cause which they must have felt strongly about: the fatwa

on Salman Rushdie which had recently been rein-
stated by the Ayotallah Khomenei. What did I think
about it? Wasn't it only right? I hadn't read *The
Satanic Verses* and hadn't yet met Salman Rushdie.
Nevertheless, I defended the freedom of the writer.
The discussion was tumultuous. The teachers seemed
to be more in favour of the fatwa than their students.
I had nothing to lose in that obscure college faced
with persons of little importance but I was glad I had
the courage to express openly my opinion.

When Time of the Writer closed, Richard and I
planned to spend a few days in Johannesburg. But
such an idea raised a general protest. Were we mad?
Johannesburg had become one of the most violent
and dangerous places in the world. Since the end
of apartheid, the whites had fled; their villas and
apartments were now occupied as squats by the
unemployed, drug dealers and all kinds of criminal
characters. Bodies piled up every day at the crossoads.

This apocalyptic picture scared us. We were
wondering what to do when the French cultural services, very active in South Africa, offered to take
charge of all the French-speaking writers provided
they took part in the Francophonie Festival in
Johannesburg. Despite my mistrust of the word
'Francophonie', I had no choice but to accept their
proposition.

We were therefore piled into a villa in the suburb
of Melville where the rooms were arranged around
a tiny swimming pool. Starting at dawn, we could

hear the servants chatter, quarrel and scream with laughter. In the evening, a team of security guards settled down on the pavement and noisily played cards. The only moment of peace and quiet was breakfast time. Ahmadou Kourouma, who suffered from insomnia and wrote all night long, would read us pages from his future novel *Allah Is Not Obliged*. He was already very frail. Nevertheless, he kept intact his sense of humour, his politeness and his extreme simplicity.

'Invite me to your university in America,' he teased me. 'I've got lots of stories to tell, you'll see.'

I didn't have time. While I was investigating the French departments likely to be interested in his visit, I learnt the sad news that he had died.

In the villa at Melville, I had no scruples visiting the kitchen. Deeply shocked by these frequent forays, the servants looked at me stony-faced and answered in monosyllables. Yet I learnt to cook impala, kudu and ostrich stews. One of the servants who was especially hostile mumbled between her teeth a phrase which would have found favour with my mother: 'Real ladies don't bother about what to cook.'

I also learnt to cook pap which both whites and blacks consider South Africa's traditional dish. It's a porridge made with corn, garnished with tomatoes and a condiment called chakalaka.

It was difficult to stay so close to Johannesburg and not try and visit it. One day, standing it no longer, Richard and I decided to disregard the warnings.

Three taxis refused to take us. A fourth accepted, provided there would be no stopping and no visiting risky neighbourhoods. After we had reached an agreement, he padlocked the doors and wound up the windows, plunging us into a steamy heat. I didn't see much of Johannesburg except for the murky facades of abandoned buildings, their windows gaping open or crudely patched up with planks of wood. The crowds of passers-by came and went dressed in their sad rags unlike the joyfully coloured camisoles and wrappers of West Africa.

The Francophonie Festival was no more interesting than Time of the Writer. Mornings we attended book signings in bookstores that were always empty. Afternoons in libraries or media centres where nobody ever came. Ostensibly, despite the efforts of the cultural services, French was not a success in South Africa.

One great honour: we were invited to lunch by the French ambassador in his sumptuous residence in Pretoria. He was a talkative man and personal friend of Jacques Chirac. I was flattered because he had read *Segu* and compared it to a historical novel he had written which I was ashamed to say I had never heard of.

'Thomas Mofolo and his *Chaka* make for serious competitors,' he joked. 'But our books are just as good.'

During a classical meal of Rossini tournedos and fried potatoes, he described his book to me at length.

He had been fascinated by the Zulus, a nation that had fought against the English, the Afrikaans as well as other African ethnic groups. They were now reduced to dancing and spear-throwing for tourists. During the dessert of Baked Alaska, he asked me whether I would like to meet Nelson Mandela. Stunned, I stammered that I would.

'I think he would like talking with you. I'll arrange an appointment.'

For a few days I was in seventh heaven. I could at last ask Mandela the questions I felt strongly about. This terrible violence that was tearing the country apart since the end of apartheid, wasn't it partly caused by the slogans of forgiveness and reconciliation? Unable to attack their former executioners, the people were turning against each other and mutilating themselves. The threat of a civil war had to be thwarted, but weren't there other ways of doing it? Unfortunately, the conversation never took place. One morning a secretary called to say that the president's agenda was full. I came down to earth with a bump.

Following the Francophonie Festival, we had a few weeks to fill. Richard and I decided to visit the Kwa Maritane natural park. If we couldn't kill the wild animals, at least we could kill time. But there was one factor we hadn't taken into account. Until then, we had frequented groups of Africans, Europeans, Indians and Asians, and been protected by their rainbow coalition. Now, from one day to the next, we found ourselves alone. Defenceless. A white man with his black wife in a country where, until recently, such a union had been illegal.

I could read a profound hostility, even hatred, in the eyes of the whites as well as the blacks around us.

At first Richard put on a brave face. He claimed I was carried away by my imagination as a novelist. Gradually, he came to realize that the toxic atmosphere was not my imagination; it was seeping into him too.

Kwa Maritane comprised a hotel complex and a casino. In its thousand-acre park, the wild animals lived in semi-liberty. At dawn, so as to catch them at their daily routine, visitors would climb into jeeps driven by the park rangers along designated roads. I soon realized that the wild animals busy sleeping, playing and making love were less formidable than the humans. I had cold sweats every time I set foot in the dining room: at once a deathly silence fell and we were burnt by a hundred looks. The waiters, too, were reluctant to serve us. Fortunately, a magnificent buffet had been set up in a corner and we could help ourselves. We didn't dare set foot in the theatre where films, concerts and lectures were available. Once breakfast was over, we shut ourselves up in our room, jumping at the slightest noise, such as a crackling similar to the sound of a Kalashnikov, inexplicable growling and explosions. Worst were the evenings when we had to walk to the restaurant for dinner—we had to cross a vast, sparsely lit park floating with ghostly shapes. I imagined attackers behind every bush.

It was with great relief that we left Kwa Maritane and flew to Cape Town. Alas, this relief did not last long. I have attempted to depict in *The Story of the Cannibal Woman* the unforgettable impression that the city of Cape Town left on me: fascination, repulsion and terror. I hope things have changed since. But when I went there in 1998, Cape Town was white, a city of whites, made for whites. Steeped in apartheid, it cared little about the democratic changes in the country and relentlessly rejected all those it considered subalterns to the surrounding belt of townships. At night, when I left a restaurant, I imagined policemen emerging out of the dark, demanding to see my pass which I couldn't show and having me thrown into prison where I was beaten up.

On our arrival, a terrible event was making headlines. Fiela, a highly respected black woman, well liked at church and director of the Sunday choir, had murdered her husband, cut him up into tiny pieces and stored them in her refrigerator. Then she'd eaten them either as a stew or grilled on a skewer. Sometimes she made them into minced meat in the fat sausages so popular in South Africa. She had told the policemen who came to arrest her: 'Enough was enough. It was either him or me.'

The Story of the Cannibal Woman can be read as a dialogue with this terrible, enigmatic murderer. Psychiatrists, some of them from England, analysed her behaviour and said that the couple is a site for a ferocious power play in which one inevitably falls victim to the other. I couldn't believe my ears, I who had always thought that a couple walked hand in hand along the exciting road of life. What abyss, what trap lay hidden there? That face which appeared on television and on the front page of every newspaper, sombre, impenetrable, her eyes two glazed slits, her lips clenched over her carnassial teeth, began to haunt me. For forty years, Fiela had been the perfect wife, washing her husband's clothes, ironing and cooking for him until that terrible, fatal deed. What secret tensions hid behind their apparent privacy and intimacy? I then had the idea of introducing into *The Story of the Cannibal Woman* the portrait of a mixed couple, like my own, where the husband led a double life unbeknownst to his wife. She a painter, an artist, seeking to express a voice of her own.

Unlike The Time of the Writer, the conference on Black Aesthetics was fascinating. It brought together some of Africa's most prominent intellectuals, such as Françoise Verges, Achille Mbembe, his wife Sarah and sculptor Ousmane Sow. Yet all these brilliant minds were swept aside and forgotten once we met Henri de la Salle, vice-consul of France. It was not because of Marguerite Duras' novel or his sharp intelligence. But because he was the husband in a mixed couple, married to Zena, a tall, beautiful Somali woman, handsomely black and always dressed in white, as if she wanted to highlight the colour of her skin. The four of us became inseparable. Day after day, we walked up to the Mount Nelson Hotel, reputed to be one of the ten establishments serving the best afternoon tea in the world. We downed dry martinis in trendy bars, dined in the best restaurants, visited the area's vineyards and tasted some of their renowned vintage wines. Sometimes we drove as far as Cape Point to admire where the Atlantic and Indian oceans meet in a turbulent frenzy.

Zena's reactions were totally different from mine. Whereas I lived with a constant anguish and tension, she savoured the silent violence and rage we aroused everywhere we went. She would have liked someone to abuse us verbally, even physically, which would have occurred if we visited the surrounding townships instead of Cape Town's smart, residential neighbourhoods.

'We're two traitors to the race,' she delighted in saying.

I protested. I defended myself in earnest. I listed all that I had said in my books and articles.

'But who reads you?' she scoffed. 'I'm talking about the impression you make when you turn up with your white husband.'

One day she asked me to accompany her on her charity rounds, her main activity as wife of a vice-consul, handing out gifts to orphanages, daycare and disabled children's centres as well as retirement homes for the needy. I accepted without thinking, seeing it as an occasion to visit the townships from the within, the most intriguing of which was Khayelitsha, a huge swath on one side of Cape Town. Its reputation for violence had prevented me from going. But I had barely sat down on the back seat of the black limousine flying the tricolour flag than I realized I had made a mistake: I had no authority to play the role I was about to perform.

The streets of Khayelitsha were scrubbed clean: no rubbish, not a single piece of litter, not one empty bottle; merely rows of dustbins lined up on perfectly swept pavements. Well-intentioned architects had painted the maisonettes lining the streets in rainbow colours or yellow and orange, supposedly to add a cheerful touch. The public gardens were deserted, since every able-bodied person was toiling away in Cape Town. The benches were moulded into unexpected shapes: rockets, airplanes and helicopters. Flowers and multicoloured shrubs grew everywhere. Yet a heavy atmosphere of sadness reigned, as if you were walking through a high-security prison which was trying to put on a cheerful show.

At the Albert Luthuli orphanage, the children crowded into the yard, waved small tricolour flags on our arrival and sang *Frère Jacques* in plaintive voices. Zena handed out her presents. The principal hugged her and thanked her profusely. The same scene was repeated everywhere we went. After the centre for disabled children, I burst out: 'Why are you taking part in such a farce?'

'What farce?' Zena said in feigned innocence.

'You know very well these people loathe you and despise you,' I exclaimed. 'To them you're nothing but a whore.'

'Exactly,' she smiled. 'They don't dare show it. They're trapped. They cannot afford to insult a woman who represents one of their allies and brings them gifts which they greatly need.'

She gloated. She jubiliated. But I was devastated.

On the other hand, not only did Zena refuse to accompany us to Robben Island, she also tried to persuade me not to go.

'It's a horrible place,' she claimed. 'Tourist voyeurs come from all over the world to take pictures of the cell where Mandela pined away for years and take selfies in the quarries where he broke rocks. It's as if the Catholic Church lets people take photos of themselves pretending to be crucified on Golgotha. It's where people were lulled into thinking that Mandela learnt Afrikaans in order to fraternize with his jailors and elaborate his theory of reconciliation. Don't go. You won't be able to stand it.'

To Richard's great surprise I followed her advice, mainly because this visit to Cape Town had been too painful for me. I needed simple, unequivocal pleasures. To my great regret, I had to finally say farewell to Zena. Since Henri's assignment to South Africa was over, he and his family had to return to Paris. Zena and I cried our hearts out. Henri shrugged. 'Why are you crying? It's not as if you won't ever see each other again.'

I was to see Zena and Henri again in their posh apartment on the rue du Ranelagh. But France is not South Africa. Despite its shortcomings, Paris is not Cape Town. The vibrant, burning link which bonded us during those several weeks was broken. Zena had become the wife of a high-ranking French official waiting to leave for his post in Dubai. I was still a writer with no fixed address. We looked at each other as if we were strangers.

Nature abhors a vacuum. Zena and Henri were soon replaced in our hearts. The Last Resort, the bed and breakfast where we were housed, was squeezed up against an elegant one-story building where the doors and windows were left wide open onto a pleasant interior furnished with armchairs, low sofas, rocking chairs and canopied beds. By dint of bumping into them on the pavement on Camp Street, and seeing them stroll around their garden, we ended up getting to know our neighbours, Jesse and Catherine Brand. They had never really fought against apartheid, but they had never approved their government's politics either. Both musicians, she a pianist, he a flautist, they had signed multiple contracts to perform in England and the States while their two children continued their education in Geneva. They had only returned to Cape Town for good in 1994, once Nelson Mandela had been elected. At the time, they both taught in a music school founded by an English conductor who recruited singers from the townships.

One evening they invited us to go with them for a performance of Handel's Messiah. Used to the sounds of the griots, I was perplexed by these African sopranos, mezzo-sopranos, tenors, countertenors and basses. The countertenor was a slender, curly-haired mixed blood, visibly a homosexual. How does one live one's homosexuality in South Africa? I knew that Kenya's and Zimbabwe's brutal dictates did not apply here. But I imagined it couldn't be easy to grow up and live with such a sexual orientation.

Out of curiosity, I went up to him and soon we were engaged in a deep conversation. 'I learnt to sing,' he told me, 'by listening to the radio. I loved listening to opera arias. I made no distinction between Puccini, Verdi and Mozart. They were quite simply beautiful.'

One Sunday, the Brands took us for a braai in a natural park on the edge of an artificial lake. The braai, a kind of barbecue, is a national institution. It is not intended for two or even four people but a number of guests who then slice up the impala and ostrich meat which has been left to macerate for days, help barbecue it and serve it. The guests must also down a good many mugs of beer and glasses of wine and know how to sing in unison. The Brands invited two other couples who drove up in a grey four-by-four, dressed in identical shorts and flowery shirts, the women wearing floppy hats. It was the first time I found myself in the company of white South Africans. Whereas I couldn't help feeling greatly apprehensive, I was surprised to find them affable, polite and ready to make fun of everything.

'You're a writer,' exclaimed Bill, one of the husbands, 'Your husband is your translator. Look out for the domestic quarrels ahead.'

Amid the general laughter Richard and I claimed the contrary.

'Besides, she never reads my translations,' Richard specified.

'That's worse,' Shirley guffawed.

In the middle of another burst of laughter, I explained it was a mark of trust on my behalf. I was convinced that Richard could never betray my ideas.

It is this image I would have liked to keep of Cape Town and all of South Africa: a cosmopolitan group enjoying themselves and having fun, prefiguring the rainbow nation that Mandela constantly promised.

Starting from ten in the evening, all the houses in Cape Town's residential neighbourhoods were protected by security guards armed with repeating rifles. They were almost exclusively French-speaking Congolese and Rwandans. Seated on the pavement, they made mint tea and ate shrimp fritters. The one protecting The Last Resort was called Kadima. I sometimes fell into a conversation with him. He would tell me about the extreme poverty of his country, for years trampled by the boots of three rival armies, describing how the women were raped and the children whom nobody wanted were piled into makeshift orphanages. He also complained about

the South Africans' frightening xenophobia, exasperated at seeing so many immigrants land up in their
country.

'If they could kill us, they would,' he claimed.

The day before I left, he gave me a simple neck-
lace of blue beads. I have wrapped it around the neck
of a pretty wooden guinea fowl I bought in Durban.

'Something good comes out of something bad' goes the French saying and the English proverb echoes 'Every cloud has a silver lining'. Despite the fact that I had been deeply affected by my stay in South Africa, it pointed me in the direction of a new research. On leaving Cape Town, I was convinced that the best way to release what I had just experienced would be to write a novel with the city as its background. To my surprise, the notes I sketched out proved to be of little interest. I couldn't manage to construct a satisfying story, probably because in South Africa I had been neither insulted nor attacked. Everything had boiled down to looks, expressions and attitudes to which perhaps I had overreacted and taken offence. In fact, it took me several years to arrive at *The Story of the Cannibal Woman*. If I managed to write this novel, it is because I transformed it into an entirely fictional narrative, focusing on the imaginary love life of Rosélie, a painter from Guadeloupe, and her husband, an English professor. The image of Fiéla, however, the heroine of a real-life news item, never left me. Her impenetrable, stubborn face, with her heavy lids half drooping over her eyes, constantly haunted me. Because of her, I launched into my research on cannibalism.

It was autumn. The leaves had begun to change colour and there was a cool breeze in the air. I made my way back to Butler Library. American university libraries are a far cry from French libraries where grey-smocked attendants hand you the object of your research through a narrow, wire-meshed window. In America, you can ramble freely through the stacks in tall dark rooms. You can breathe in the inimitable smell of paper and leaf through books of your choosing.

I soon discovered that cannibalism is practised more often than is commonly thought. A few years earlier, to the horror of the world, a Japanese man had eaten his female companion. Following a plane crash in the Andes, the remaining passengers had eaten each other. As early as the nineteenth century, Théodore Géricault's painting *The Raft of the Medusa* can be considered an ode to cannibalism since those who remained alive on that wretched raft, deprived of food, had resorted to this sole means of survival.

It was by pure coincidence that I came across the *Manifesto antropofàgico* published in 1924 by a Brazilian, Oswaldo de Andrade. Oswald de Andrade belonged to his country's intellectual elite; he lived in France and there met André Breton, author of *The Surrealist Manifesto*. The *Manifesto antropofàgico* is an iconoclastic, derisive text, full of a play on words and bad puns on serious topics. Because of its tone and content, it instantly became my bible and I rank it among my favourite works.

Oswaldo de Andrade offered the colonized subject a brilliant solution, a unique way of solving the problem of creativity and how to live in harmony with his multiple influences. Since it was impossible to rid himself entirely of the legacy of his colonial masters, the colonized subject should imitate, metaphorically, the Tupi Indians, infamous for devouring a good many Portuguese priests bent on evangelizing them. In truth, they feasted mainly on their victims' noble parts, those which could make them stronger and more intelligent i.e. the liver, heart and brains. Likewise the colonized are invited to choose among the Western values imposed upon them, to select only those which can lead to their enrichment. To operate such a selection requires enormous lucidity: gone the idolizing respect and servile attachment to the ideas instilled by the colonizer. The Cannibal Manifesto was both a satirical therapy and an in-depth reflection on the complexity of postcolonial literature.

I became even more excited when I discovered that Oswaldo de Andrade's companion was a well-known painter. This meant that the theory of cannibalism was valid for every type of artistic creation. Once I delved into my research, I gave a great deal of thought to the theory I had discovered. I called it literary cannibalism, an unusual, even shocking, metaphor. The term aroused the curiosity of the departments of francophone studies who were used to dealing with the somewhat worn-out concepts of Negritude and Créolité. I was treated to an excellent article in the widely read *Journal of Higher Education*. I was invited to speak on numerous university campuses, some of them highly respected. The French Department at Princeton organized a conference on the subject where I was the guest of honour, in the company of eminent professors such as philosopher Anthony Appiah. In short, without being big-headed, I had everything going my way and got the impression I was leading a charmed life.

I was invited to Saint Michael's College in a pleasant region, wide open to the horizon on the Chesapeake Bay. Just as I was about to speak in the crowded amphitheatre, a group of young Africans or African Americans, I couldn't say which, burst into the room. The boys had their heads wrapped in those horrible hoods which black youths are so fond of in order to look fearsome and scary. They settled down noisily in the back row. I had barely finished speaking when one of them stood up and introduced himself: Adoremus Bokandé from Rwanda. The word 'cannibal', he said, could not have a positive connotation since it alluded to a custom that the Africans had been wrongly accused of. The theory of literary cannibalism was not only devoid of meaning, it was also extremely dangerous.

I am used to criticism. But what revolted me was the students' prolonged applause following his speech. It was typical of American scholars: scared of being accused of racism and prepared to find favour with the wildest flights of fancy. I endeavoured to keep calm. It was obvious Adoremus hadn't understood a thing. It wasn't a question of actual or imagined cannibalism by the Africans, but by the Tupi Indians that Oswaldo de Andrade was referring to. The discussion became disorderly and I wasn't sure I had the last word. At the end of the lecture, Adoremus came up to me, handed me his business card and asked for an appointment.

To cut a long story short, I'll say that Adoremus soon became a close friend, which shouldn't come as a surprise. In America, relationships between professor and student are very different from those in France; they are often more intimate and friendly.

Since Adoremus made frequent visits to New York, I invited him to our apartment on Riverside Drive where he told me his terrible story. When he was around five or six, a troop from a rival ethnic group marched into the church where he was attending mass with his parents. They machine-gunned anything that moved, then left after padlocking the exits. For four days, Adoremus lay under the cold and increasingly heavy bodies of his parents who had fallen on top of him like a protective shield. Then he had been picked up by an NGO and passed around from orphanage to study centre before landing up in the States.

He was not very cheerful company, in all honesty, and never stopped talking about the genocide in Rwanda which in the end bored Richard and our guests. But he took advantage of my weak point:

cooking. He would turn up unexpectedly, his arms loaded with brown-paper bags crammed with all sorts of ingredients he would then use to make savoury dishes. He specialized in yam-and-sweet-potato au gratin which he garnished with fish balls served in a sweet-and-sour sauce, mixed with vinegar, tamarind and hot pepper. I watched admiringly as his large, bony hands dressed the meat and wondered how he had acquired such skill and knowledge in a field reserved exclusively for women in Africa.

When I asked him, he sighed: 'If I tell you my life, you'll turn it into a novel. The NGO handed me over to the owner of a cheap restaurant in Kigali. I became her whipping boy. She would pinch me to the bone if I didn't chop the onions and herbs fine enough. To punish me, she made me swallow hot pepper.'

When he came to New York on a Saturday evening, he would often take Richard and me to the African American nightclubs in Brooklyn. We would go down to the very lower end of the city and travel over the black waters of the East River on a suspension bridge. I liked accompanying him to those clubs. For the space of a few hours, I could dream I was losing myself in the African American community that had become so inaccessible to me. Adoremus was on first name terms with everyone. He was friends with the rappers and played the guitar, flute and saxophone. He would try and drag me onto the dance floor. 'Come on,' he would insist. 'Let yourself go.'

I couldn't let myself go since I could hear my mother's words whistling around my ears and poking fun at the cliché of how blacks have dancing in their blood. My body would grow rigid and I would be invaded by notions of decency, elegance and decorum.

The only thing I hated was when Adoremus asked me for money. He constantly borrowed twenty or thirty or fifty dollars which he promised to pay back but never did. It was as if he forgot from one week to the next. In order to calm my annoyance, I would tell myself that I earned ten times more than he did and in so doing I was paying back the debt to the Third World. I had grown up in a family where sharing was common practice. My mother handed out to needy and illegitimate children a good share of her income. But when Adoremus asked me for five hundred dollars, I refused outright.

He stared at me in contempt. 'That's just like the bourgeoisie,' he said. 'Always stingy.'

It was the only time we came close to breaking up.

Winter was drawing to a close. Buds began to sprout on the branches of the trees in Central Park. We exchanged our long, heavy overcoats for lighter clothes. One day, I found a badly printed flyer in my mailbox: the Gethsemane Association welcomed every informed African and African American student to its next meeting which this year coincided with Easter Sunday. Debate topic: to put a stop to Profes-

sor Maryse Condé's dangerous theory of literary cannibalism. There followed a list of speakers headed by
Adoremus Bokandé. My heart skipped a beat. Why
had Adoremus never mentioned it? Ever since he'd
become a frequent visitor to Riverside Drive, we had
never tackled the subject of literary cannibalism. I
thought the hatchet had been definitely buried. This
resurgence had all the trappings of treason. Then my
inherent optimism took the upper hand and I
endeavoured to minimize the impact. Who had ever
heard of the Gethsamene Association? Was it a secular or religious association? Who did Adoremus
Bokandé think he was? A young pup of no importance, an employee under contract to teach Swahili
in the flimsy programme of African languages at
Saint Michael's. No intellectual heavyweight.

Then I wondered what attitude to adopt. Should
I pretend to ignore the matter? Or should I go to the
Bronx where this Gethsamene Association had its
offices and stand up to my potential disparagers? If
there was one thing I never envisioned, it was to let
Richard in on my concerns. I knew he would disap-
prove since he never thought much of Adoremus. I
spent the night meditating. It would have been
absurd to think I was secretly attracted to Adoremus.
First, he was far from being an Adonis. Then, as I
have already said, I was the faithful wife of one man.
It would have been absurd too to think that I had
taken Adoremus to be my son whose image my
memory had made sacred. It was more likely that I
had been blinded by an unconscious paternalism

towards this Third World which Adoremus symbolized to perfection. Living affluently so far from people of my own colour never failed to fill me with a feeling of guilt, which explained the flaws in my behaviour and my lack of lucidity. I spent the following days calling Adoremus, sending emails and text messages. To no avail. I don't know how it would have all ended if one afternoon some students hadn't knocked on my office door: a motley group of devoted students from Columbia but also an assortment of boys and girls from universities where I had lectured. They were all aware of the meeting the Gethsamene Association was planning. They offered to go and defend me, for they considered I had been misunderstood and attacked unfairly.

We agreed on the position I would adopt: stay on the sidelines and take no part in this quarrel which was probably dictated out of jealousy.

'The Rwandans are wicked,' Carija, a young Congolese, sighed. 'Look what the Hutus did to the Tutsis.'

During the weeks that followed, Adoremus remained invisible. He made no attempt to get in touch nor did he show up at Riverside Drive. I must confess I considered this unilateral breach in our relations as an infliction of suffering. After Easter Sunday, the loyal students came back to report: they had castigated my detractors who had been incompetent and incapable of establishing a valid theory. Even more surprising, Adoremus had been absent.

They had no idea where he was. Their questions about him had remained unanswered. Out of curiosity, I got in touch with the head of the Department of African Languages at St Michael's and learnt that Adoremus Bokandé, the contract worker, had exchanged his job as a teacher for that of a better-paid job as security guard at a bank in Wilmington. A bank? Which bank? The department knew nothing more. I realized that trying to find Adoremus would be like looking for a needle in a haystack. In the end, I brought myself to accept it.

But in light of this event I took great care to remind my students that cannibalism was a vice attributed without proof whatsoever to the Africans and to the indigenous peoples of the Caribbean. Christopher Columbus had never been able to describe these 'cannibal feasts' which were supposed to take place throughout the islands. The theory of literary cannibalism was based solely on the Tupi Indians whose anthropological rites had been authenticated by historians.

In June, I received a postcard depicting a newborn, comical and fragile as they all are, its eyes closed under a woollen bonnet. Adoremus Bokandé and Zora Williamson were pleased to announce the birth of their son, Déogratias.

Déogratias, indeed!

I accepted the invitation of the International Congress of Francophone Studies not because the programme was particularly original or promising, and not because I was going to be given an obscure literary prize whose name I have forgotten, but because it was being held in Romania. I could therefore put my obsession with Africa temporarily on the backburner. As my problems with Adoremus amply demonstrated, Africa remained an enigma to me. I still didn't understand a thing. In Romania, they would talk about Count Dracula, vampires and how they feigned sleep in crypts and woke up lusting for blood. I recalled Roman Polanski's *The Fearless Vampire Killers* and Werner Herzog's *Nosferatu*, two films that had made a deep impression on me. I like fantastical tales. One of my favourite novels is unquestionably Mary Shelley's *Frankenstein*, the crazy story of a creature that escapes the grip of its creator. This relationship comes to light in my novel *Who Slashed Célanire's Throat*, where Dr Jean Pinceau is an avatar of the famous scientist; and in *Les Belles Ténébreuses*, where the couple formed by Ramzi and Kassem has a strange relationship with the corpses they are in charge of embalming.

Despite detesting all forms of violence, I must confess I have, strangely enough, always been fascinated by blood. Looking back, I wonder what obscure ground bred my attraction to literary cannibalism. When my brothers and sisters and I were children, Adélia used to coagulate ox blood for us with a handful of cooking salt—in order to prevent anemia. She would then cut it up into thick slices, fry it and serve it seasoned with small onions and *figs* (as green bananas are called).

As we left the airport at Bucharest, everything was suddenly transformed into the setting for an operetta. Not a cloud or a shadow in a sky as blue as a child's drawing. The sun beamed good-naturedly. Since the congress was to be held in the small town of Sibiu two hours away, the participants fanned out into three antiquated coaches which set off in single file along a semi-deserted road stretching away as far as the eye could see. The only vehicles we passed were horse-drawn carts driven by men in corduroy suits, seated beside fair-haired children and women with flowery scarves. Farm buildings emerged in the middle of meadows where oxen grazed on thick grass. It was a bucolic landscape, as if we had gone back in time, as if we had turned back the clock.

Sibiu was situated in the Carpathian Mountains, which meant that suddenly the road began to climb and an unexpected chill descended. It was a pretty little town, a picture-postcard town: richly built houses encircled a mediaeval church; the streets were crowded with people but very few cars; and the same old-fashioned atmosphere reigned.

The hotel for the participants was located in the midst of a thick wood straight out of Hansel and Gretel. For the opening ceremony, the organizers had planned an evening of folklore, for singing and music in Romania were very much alive, and, unlike the rest of the world, had not been corrupted by Anglo-Saxon influences. First, a choir entered the stage and broke into a series of harmonious songs. Then a quartet played some gypsy music, followed by a full orchestra complete with accordionists and saxophonists, dancers that reminded me of Russian acrobats and more choirs singing a cappella. This went on for hours. Then the speeches began. The officials were keen to point out that Romania, although not a French-speaking country, was close to the spirit and flavour of France as witnessed by the number of visitors between the two countries.

I was beginning to get bored when the mayor of Sibiu, cramped into traditional costume which obviously he seldom wore, announced the start of the banquet. In the next door room, heavy but delicious dishes were being served: sausages, pâtés, meat stews, cabbage and potatoes. I thought the desserts too sweet, especially the Turkish delight and the strange pink pastries. It was almost two in the morning before the evening was over and the official cars spluttered back to town.

It was only on Day Four that a visit to Count Dracula's castle was planned. Up till then, the presentations had been interspersed by brief excursions which had shown us the splendour of the Romanian landscape and the beauty of its towns. The congress had remained true to form: individual presentations limited to forty minutes and general discussions. Sometimes a documentary brightened up the humdrum proceedings. I attended a round table devoted to my work and, as usual, couldn't see myself in the analyses I heard. How come I was portrayed as a rebellious and nomadic writer but not a commendable one? Was it because I had dared to criticize Negritude? Was it because I had dared to express my opinion on Créolité? I had done so with no intention to hurt or shock—I was merely giving my version of the truth. But perhaps that's what 'rebellious' means? Tell one's truth come what may.

It's considered good taste to talk about Romania in a patronizing fashion, and the colleagues seated at our table never failed to do so. Romania was underdeveloped. You only had to look at the way the fields were cultivated. No tractors, no trucks; only old-fashioned tools such as scythes and ploughs. It was obvious the country had not made the great leap forward which proved how useless, and even harmful, Communism had been.

'What's your opinion after having lived in a number of Marxist countries?' one of the participants asked

I attempted to explain that I had lived in regimes where a dictatorship had hidden behind the mask of Marxism. Matters could be truly different if, in a perspective of genuine socialism, leaders took the interests of their people to heart.

'Unfortunately, that has never happened anywhere,' scoffed my neighbour.

I would have liked to protest and launch into a peremptory and scathing response, but, given the facts, it was out of the question and so I chose to keep peeling my pear in silence.

The visit to Bran, the castle of Vlad the Impaler, Count Dracula, did not make a lasting impression on me. I have visited many castles, both in England and in France. One of our friends owns a castle in Normandy where we have spent many a weekend. It belonged to his father who made his fortune by inventing curling tongs. Despite this dubious origin, the castle was an impressive one, with its series of connecting rooms, huge fireplaces and turrets. Dracula's castle was balanced on the side of a hill. Walking through the garden, you got the impression of hanging over a void. The interior was loaded with mirrors, heavy dark-red drapes, suits of armour and weapons from every century. Although it wasn't the height of the tourist season, the visitors crowded in, eager to take pictures. They were mainly Europeans content to dive back into the past, nurtured by the legends of vampires in Transylvania, the subject of so many films and novels. There was also the inevitable quota of Japanese.

At the foot of the castle, a market spread out over a huge square as merry as a fairground. All sorts of handmade items were on sale: embroidered blouses and dresses, richly brocaded velvet jackets, leather shorts, boots as well as straw and felt hats. Beneath small tents set up around the square, waitresses wearing comical flounced skirts and waiters close-fitted in costumes resembling that of a gamekeeper, were busy serving coffee and pastries. I started up a conversation with a Dutch couple seated nearby. It all began with the inevitable questions about Guadeloupe and how Richard and I had met. The conversation then turned to more general subjects.

'Have you visited Bucharest?' the young woman asked.

I said we were attending a congress and wouldn't be free to visit the city until the end of the week.

'It's the most horrible place you can imagine. The People's Palace built by Ceausecu is hideous, like most of the administrative buildings. Poor Romanians! Lacking money to pull it all down, they are forced to live with such an ugly capital.'

We exchanged business cards, as Richard and I often visited Amsterdam to see our friend Mineke Schipper whom I met at *Présence Africaine*. As the result of a bad fall while cycling with my children in Kaolack, I could no longer mount a bicycle. I never tired, however, of walking along the canals, admiring the silky reflection of the water and the elegant, narrow, rectilinear facades of the merchants' houses. I also liked roaming the red-light district where the prostitutes sat in full view in their windows.

After the castle, we set off for Brasov, Sibiu's rival. Both towns compete for the role of Romania's tourist capital. A cultural association had organized a ball in our honour. A ball! The very name brings to mind an incident of insulting behaviour I have never forgotten. When I was a teenager, I let myself be dragged off sometimes to the Bal Titane, as the alcohol-free parties organized for young people in the afternoon were called. As a rule, they took place in the Jeanne d'Arc parish hall. I didn't dance for the reasons I have already given. I would eat paper cones of peanuts and goblets of coconut sorbet. The boys paid me little attention, which was agony for me. Was my mother right? Was I ugly and ungainly? Today I realize there were two reasons for their lack of interest. One: I was too tall. At fourteen, I was already almost five and a half feet tall. Such a height scared off any eventual partners. Two: my colour. I was black in an island where the men preferred light-skinned girls. My education, however, forbade me to confront that reason or to take it into serious consideration. Only years later was I forced to do so and discovered that my parents, although they had a high opinion of themselves, in the eyes of some people, nevertheless, remained black.

One afternoon, one of the boys insisted I accompany him onto the dance floor. His name was Iko Blanchard and he was a junior, I believe, at the Lycée

Carnot. He was very black and not at all handsome; his face was marked with an enormous scar which contorted his right eye, and I was somewhat ashamed that such a sorry figure was all I could come up with. He was an excellent dancer, masterful and self-assured. I did my best to follow him. I thought I had managed to do so when I heard chuckling behind my back. Disconcerted, I turned round to face a group who were in stitches watching me.

'Bravo, Mademoiselle, you do know how to shake your booty!' one of them said ironically in Creole.

Thereupon the others burst out laughing. Their mockery pierced me like Saint Sebastian's arrows. I let go of Iko's hand, made a dash for the exit and ran back home. Then I collapsed on my bed and sobbed tears of humiliation.

This galling image of a ball remained engraved in my memory. It was only counterbalanced years later when, on the recommendation of Ina Césaire, I attended a remarkable performance by Compagnie du Compagnol of a play called *Le Bal*, directed by Jean-Claude Penchenat, which illustrated through the medium of dance how our society had developed over the years.

The ball at Brasnov was very much like the Bals Titanes of my youth. Rows of chairs and pedestal tables had been placed on three sides of a floodlit, rectangular room. A large platform had been set up on the fourth side where sat the musicians in full costume. The mayor of Brasnov, also in traditional costume, gave the signal for the festivities to begin by embracing one of his female assistants; then the entire town council followed suit. It was not a place for airs and graces nor for pampering the wounds inherited from childhood. It was a place where you let yourself go and you couldn't afford to be finicky. But I was unable to get a hold of myself and fled to the balcony instead. Down below in the garden, decorated with coloured lanterns and lights, tables had been set up and an accordionist was playing softly. I went downstairs where waiters were serving heaps of refreshments: pastries stuffed with meat, sausages and almond cakes. I wasn't at all hungry. But between eating and dancing, I had little choice.

Two days later was the closing ceremony of the congress. Naturally, it was another occasion for a concert of traditional music. It's a well-known fact, conferences are places for bringing participants closer by creating or strengthening ties between them. They are made to feel as long-standing friends. Is it because they live in close proximity for several days at a time? It's not unusual at the end of a congress to see participants leave in tears. After the conference, most of the participants took advantage of a visit to central Europe. One group planned to travel to Istanbul, attracted by this city and its reputation as Pearl of the Bosphorus. Today, I regret we didn't join them since Orham Pamuk, forced into exile, now teaches at Columbia and has got us interested in that part of the world through its literature.

Richard and I decided to spend one or two nights in Bucharest. The city deserves its reputation. The People's Palace is said to be the biggest monument in Europe. In order to build it, fifty thousand families were thrown into the street by the communist regime. A guide who raced us through its countless rooms told us all that in a casual tone of voice. However far we wandered through the streets of Bucharest, we were unable to find a single district that was appealing. All we could see were lines of concrete buildings, monolithic and inelegant.

The French ambassador's residence, however, was situated in an exquisitely elegant palace. It was said to date from the end of the nineteenth century when Romanian architects travelled in large numbers to Paris to soak up the splendours of the City of Light. On the walls, icons smiling out from their precious frames rubbed shoulders with rich drapes.

'I hope you liked Romania,' the ambassador asked with a smile.

He had invited us for a light lunch of quiche and salad which made a change from the solid dishes we had downed in Sibiu.

'It's a brave country, full of resources,' he continued. 'Look how it's emerged from the abyss of Communism!'

This time I couldn't keep quiet.

'Must Communism always be equated with an abyss?' I protested. 'Can't it bring happiness to the people?'

'Tell me where this has occurred,' he said calmly.

This conversation with an ambassador of a capitalist country on the benefits of socialism may seem unusual. But I had to try out my claws on an intelligent and competent speaker who did not share my opinion.

'I know what you think,' the ambassador retorted. 'I've read your articles and am fully aware you're in favour of independence. But what would independence bring to Guadeloupe?'

On second thoughts, I told myself this was not the place to engage in a discussion on politics and so I changed the conversation to the country's abundant cultural treasures that had made such an impression on us. I blame myself for being such a coward.

The ambassador was a music lover and well informed of Romania's musical diversity. He owned an extraordinary collection of records and had us listen to some Lautari, the traditional groups of popular gypsy music. He professed to have a deep admiration for Gheorghe Zamfir.

It was almost 6 p.m. before that impromptu concert came to an end.

This visit to Romania achieved its purpose. For a short time, Africa became a literary object which I sensed through the imagination of its writers. In Romania there had been no aggression. I hadn't been forced to commit an apparent act of generosity which in the end would turn against me as had occurred with Adoremus.

Before returning to the States, I accompanied Richard to Tenterden in the south of England to see his mother. For me, London is like Paris. It's a city where I always dread meeting the person I once was and reliving my anguish, my hurt and my despair. I avoided taking the Underground, scared of finding myself face to face with the young woman loaded down with a heavy briefcase, attempting to avoid thinking of her children's whining and heading bravely to Bush House and the BBC. The words Shepherds Bush, Hampstead and Golders Green on the buses terrified me as they recalled the journeys I used to take.

I liked Kent, however, that region to the south, a little less rainy than the rest of England, green and wooded. It is sprinkled with small villages huddled around their church and pub, straight out of a book of old illustrations. But, unfortunately, becoming increasingly popular with tourists year after year. The roads, so narrow that two cars had trouble passing, cut across fields of hops and mustard recognizable by their rich colour of saffron. Sometimes riders mounted on horses emerged out of the unknown and galloped in front of the car.

I wasn't interested in the memory of Dickens who lived in Kent, even if loyal members of his association were actively organizing fêtes, literary afternoons and contests. I was interested in its cuisine. On

Sundays, we went for lunch to the village of Elham, to the Abbot's Fireside . It had everything: the monumental fireplace roaring with enormous logs in winter; exposed, black varnished oak beams; tables covered with white damask cloths; heavy silverware; and seasonal flowers. It was full of local customers and offered a wide choice of carved roast meats: pork, beef and lamb garnished with the indispensable vegetables cooked in the English fashion. All washed down with local wines, as England had begun wine-growing and was producing excellent vintages.

Marjorie, Richard's mother, was not to be outdone. She was an expert cook. Her shepherd's pies, Yorkshire puddings and beef tongue were proof that there existed an English cuisine. When I offered to take over in the kitchen, she categorically refused. Richard ended up admitting that she didn't appreciate my mixtures and had been deeply shocked that I had mixed pork with mint sauce. Mint sauce goes with a leg of lamb. Full stop.

When we returned to New York in October, we arrived right in the middle of the Indian summer. I had discovered quite by chance years earlier the splendour of an Indian summer. At the start of my career, shortly after *Heremakhonon* was published, I was invited by Hedi Bouraoui for a talk at York University in Toronto. Since he probably had very little money for the invitation, he paid for my airfare to Montreal and had me travel by train for the remainder of the journey. Huddled in my compartment, I fell asleep as soon as we left Montreal. Opening my eyes a few hours later, I couldn't fathom what was happening outside—everything had been transformed. The train was running alongside a forest whose foliage blazed red, orange and yellow, something I had never seen before. Were they really trees or a decor of a strange nature? What fairy had waved her magic wand over them?

The man sitting opposite me must have seen the wonder on my face. 'It's the Indian summer. Didn't you know?'

'Indian summer?' I repeated, flabbergasted. 'What does that mean?'

'It's the last burst of summer before winter sets in.'

I got out of the train my head spinning with colours. Toronto is known for its skyscrapers and ultra-modern buildings, a city firmly in the present with immigrants from every place in the world. They speak Russian, German as well as Turkish and Arabic. York University, however, was in a calm, old-fashioned district straight out of a corner of England. You could be in Folkestone, Brighton or Eastbourne minus the sea. The trees on the pavement were all dressed in that foliage which continued to amaze me. I walked as if in a dream.

Hedi Bouraoui was a tall North African with a gaunt face who had lived for almost twenty years in Canada but had kept intact his warm manners. He welcomed me as a sister. Moreover, he had liked *Heremakhonon* very much and had shared his appreciation with his students. The following evening, the room was full for my lecture, the atmosphere was convivial and the friendly question-and-answer session lasted a long time. We then had dinner at his home where a caterer had delivered a mullet couscous, a dish immortalized by the famous film *The Secret of the Grain* directed by Abdellatif Kechiche. And so it deserves to be. The mullet is a somewhat second-rate fish whose flesh is firm and white. Once it is blended with the spices of the couscous, however, and especially mint leaves, a kind of transmutation operates and it becomes sublime.

I told Hedi Bouraoui what I felt. He shook his head. 'What a pity you don't know how to eat with your hand. It would taste even better.'

WALTZING MATILDA

Starting from the year 2000, my life began to change. My visits abroad slowed down as long flights began to tire me out. I recall in disbelief the time when I would go directly from the airport to the university to meet my colleagues, lead a discussion and perhaps join them for a meal. That time was well and truly over. I now needed almost an entire day to regain some semblance of vitality and condition my intellectual faculties. I could see in the mirror how my appearance had changed. My hair was becoming white and I had dark shadows under my eyes. My skin, once celebrated by my mother as 'soft as a sapodilla', the only part of my body she didn't denigrate, had become dull and leathery. I felt the anguish which grips all of us on seeing the shadow of old age weigh heavy on us.

In my case, the anxiety common to all humans was doubly worrisome. Wasn't my deteriorating health due to something else? I consulted specialists in New York and Paris who all came up with the same verdict: the Boucolon illness, as we liked to nickname it in order to attenuate its formidable reality, was slowly ganging up on me. Incurable and cunning, it would gradually destroy my balance, my mobility and the coordination of my movements. It would make my writing illegible. It would attack my elocution and distort my pretty voice I was so proud of. To tell the truth, I wasn't surprised. Why would it spare me? It had carried off Sandrino at the age of twenty, and, later on, a good many of my brothers and sisters as well as nephews.

Although I lost my status by travelling less, my classes gained in familiarity. They became venues loaded with friendship and places for discussing writers and literature. Student presentations were never followed up by tense or aggressive discussions as is sometimes the case. Even the shyest of students dared give an opinion. I had achieved a kind of maternal status.

In December, Richard and I travelled to Guadeloupe to spend Christmas there as usual. The journey seemed to be getting harder every year. We had to change planes in San Juan and take an ATR on American Eagle; they regularly mislaid our baggage and then delivered to us in the middle of the night. But I wouldn't have missed celebrating Christmas in Montebello for the world. Oddly enough, I had no qualms turning my back for a time on the illuminations in New York, the glittering Christmas tree at the Rockefeller Center and the noisy, bustling crowds along its avenues. The stay in Guadeloupe made for a digression into darkness and lethargy which enabled me to better understand myself. We were always on our own for Christmas Eve. My brother, sister-in-law and their offspring, for reasons I never understood, no longer came to visit. José and the patriots seldom stopped by. Sony Rupaire's death had grieved me enormously. Only my children and grandchildren came from Paris. Without bothering about their preferences, I insisted on cooking a traditional meal. I spurned the smoked salmon and oysters that were easily available in the shops at Pointe-à-Pitre and insisted on having black pudding made with pig's blood and not the conch or codfish imitations now in fashion. I had to have Creole ham, pakala yams and fresh-picked pigeon peas. The only concessions I made were Bollinger champagne and the Yule log. The latter almost disappeared from the menu when I discovered one year a pastry cook in Morne Rouge who specialized in traditional cakes. I ordered a tart of pink papayas. From the faces Richard and my children made, I realized I had made the wrong choice. Since mass was no longer celebrated at midnight—too much violence—we sat out on the terrace open to the smells and music of the night. On the other side of the bay, the lights of Le Gosier glittered in the distance. From time to time, the wind wafted in the sounds of Haitian orchestras such as Carimi or Haitian Troubadour, from brilliantly illuminated neighbouring houses where the dancing was going strong.

A few days after Christmas, in accordance with a long-standing tradition, we were paid a visit by all the children of Montebello who brought us oranges and mandarins; we had to carefully keep the pips for fear of running out of money during the year.

We would return to New York on Martin Luther King Day, in mid-January.

In 2002, among the impressive pile of mail awaiting me at Columbia on my return, I found a letter from the University of Western Australia at Perth. The president of the Association of French Studies invited Richard, my translator, and me for a conference. She obviously had trouble financing our plane tickets, so she had resorted to a number of sponsors. Thus, the English Department invited us to take part in a study symposium in New Norcia while the Maritime Museum in Freemantle requested a lecture on the Middle Passage. I recognized the hand of Bonnie Thomas whom I had hosted at Montebello the previous year. Passionate about Antillean culture, she had attended numerous *lewoz* dances and even bought the Assimil method to learn Creole.

Australia? It was so far away that I had never thought about it. Like everyone else, I had admired pictures of the white sails of the Sydney Opera House and seen a few films, *Picnic at Hanging Rock* and *A Cry in the Dark*, but none of them had made a lasting impression.

I let myself be convinced by Richard who was burning with enthusiasm to visit this former English colony, once a refuge for convicts. Then I bought a few guidebooks and half-heartedly read the story of the Aboriginal Australians. Nothing very original. The story of the indigenous peoples of Australia resembled that of all the indigenous peoples ravaged, hounded and defeated by the discoverers from the West.

In July, we travelled halfway around the globe to arrive in Perth, a city neither beautiful nor ugly, with nothing original about it except for the sun. The sky stretched blue above our heads, more intense than in Europe, dotted with puffy white clouds. What struck me while I walked along the wide streets crisscrossed at right angles and lined with identical buildings were the countless numbers of Asians. They were everywhere, in the offices, the banks, the shops and parks, queuing up in front of the cinemas. Somewhat surprised, I broached the subject with Bonnie with whom we were having dinner in a Thai restaurant.

'We have everyone here,' she replied. 'Chinese, Vietnamese, North and South Koreans, Indonesians and Filipinos.'

I couldn't make out what she was thinking by the sound of her voice. Was she pleased about this influx or did she deplore it?

She herself was of English origin and married to a French man. I loved this mismatch of alliances between individuals, this blurring of identities constantly impaired by the blows dealt by love and sex.

We had to get up very early the next morning to travel to the Maritime Museum in Freemantle. It was a magnificent building, and so wide open to the ocean that you felt the ships could sail right in. At lunch, I met Françoise Verges who was working on the project of a museum on Réunion Island, the brainchild of her father, and we decided to visit the town. Freemantle had been built by former convicts brought over from England. Its major sites were the prison, the Round House and the Immigration Museum. We had lunch on the terrace of an old-fashion hotel complete with misted antique mirrors in heavy copper frames and black-and-white-striped armchairs and sofas. The waiter insisted we try the oysters, a mollusc I have never really liked. Unless they are stuffed, as they are in the American South, but that's considered a heresy by connoisseurs.

The next day was the start of the conference of French Studies at the University of Western Australia in Perth. When I had finished speaking, Beverley, a well-known literary critic from Jamaica who worked on Edouard Glissant and whose many articles I had read, came over and invited Richard and me to dinner at her home.

'I've not cooked a Caribbean meal,' she said as she welcomed us. 'It's Australian, since the fish here are excellent.'

'And the wines too,' added her husband, Anton. 'I expect you've heard of them. They're beginning to get a name for themselves internationally.'

Anton was English, and the twenty years spent in Australia had affected little his accent and his manner. It was a hearty meal composed of an excellent fish called barramundi and a mushroom pie.

Suddenly, over dessert, Beverley told us a terrible story. Her sister had married one of the leaders of the coup d'état in Grenada in 1983. She had been jailed and for years her family had never been allowed to visit. I could see why there was a shadow deep in Beverley's grey eyes and a nervousness behind her smiles. I stammered a few words of sympathy.

'Every night,' Beverley continued, 'I dream of her. The current government of Grenada has promised to free her at last. I'm optimistic.'

Needless to say, the atmosphere grew grim and our parting was somewhat sad.

Australia only began to come to life in my eyes a few days later, when we travelled to New Norcia for the English Department's Studies Days. Mary Olson boasted of her convict ancestors and I learnt with amazement that an aristocracy had been fabricated around these convict forefathers. I thought of my parents who would never have understood taking pride in such a thing, since they prudishly threw a veil over their African origins.

New Norcia was the seat of a religious colony of Benedictine monks. It was located about 200 kilometres from Perth, in a barren region studded with prickly bushes and gigantic cacti. A wide tarred road ran through the centre. At night, the never-ending trucks or Road Trains, illuminated like cruise ships, drove through at full speed, creating whirlwinds of dust and shaking the walls of the humble monastery where the participants were housed. They were heading for Broome, capital of the pearl industry where 80 per cent of the world's mother-of-pearl is made.

Up till very recently, New Norcia was home to two orphanages for aboriginal children. In fact, the conference's guests of honour, Anne and Jonas, were two former pupils from the orphanage. They reminded me of the Indians in Guadeloupe but their skin was darker and their features more pronounced and rugged.

At first sight, they appeared to be cold and somewhat arrogant but I soon realized they were merely intimidated by the stir everybody was making around them. They were fussed over with devotion. Journalists from Perth took pictures and requested interviews. Anne was a painter whose paintings unfortunately I never got to know. Politically militant, she had also made a name for herself as a writer. She and Jonas had recounted the dark story of their childhood in popular magazines. Since their fathers were white, both of them had been snatched from their aboriginal families and placed in institutions designed to instil in them the benefits of Western civilization. Anne had accepted the system as best she could. But Jonas had always been a rebel. At fourteen, he had escaped to join his family. He had been caught and brought back to the orphanage *manu militari*. In their presentations they described those terrible years they had lived without affection, without tenderness, under the pitiless gaze of a God who seemed wanting in compassion. The audience wept listening to them. Hypocrisy? I wondered.

Anne and Jonas joined Richard and myself for lunch.

'If you want to get to know us,' Anne said, 'you'll have to come up to the so-called Northern Territory, to Alice Springs. You can stay at my place. My house is big enough.'

Unfortunately, it was out of the question. After New Norcia, we had to fly to Sydney where I had accepted to speak at the French Cultural Centre. Furthermore, we were determined to spend an evening at the Opera. And we were going to meet up with our friend Régine Cuzin who was in Australia after a visit to New Zealand.

'What a pity,' Jonas said regretfully. 'Alice Springs is our cultural capital. It's full of painters, sculptors, musicians and all sorts of artists.'

'However hard they tried,' Anne commented sadly, 'to steal everything from us, they never managed to steal our creativity.'

On the last day a farewell banquet brought us all together, although the word 'banquet' is somewhat exaggerated for the frugal dinner that was served up: fish, potatoes and oysters which seemed to be the region's pride and joy.

Two plates of lettuce were placed before Anne and Jonas. 'We're not vegetarians,' Anne explained. 'But we only eat the animals we know: the kangaroo, for example. You need years to get to know our cuisine. The term "Bush Tucker", which I don't know how to translate, refers to the meats, berries and herbs that feed us.'

I was so sorry to say goodbye since I had so very little time to get to know them. I got the impression I was missing out on the essential part of my visit. I had given it very little thought but suddenly I realized they were the perfect illustration of the disaster perpetrated by the colonial oppressor. Stripped of their land, they wandered like ghosts, despised by everyone. In spite of it all, they were a triumph for humanity since they survived as best they could. It was with a heavy heart that I flew off the following day.

In Sydney, we were housed in a brand-new, ultra-modern hotel where everything was red and black. In the rooms, the beds stretched out under black sheets and scarlet pillows. The tables and armchairs were bright red whereas an L-shaped sofa was black and deep as a tomb. Altogether, it was both appealing and somewhat scary.

We went out to visit the city.

Madeleine Hage, my teaching colleague at University of Maryland, had told me about Sydney. She said it was a city made for young people and the body beautiful. I felt exactly the same. An elegant crowd was filling the streets and the avenues alongside the sea which stretched as far as the horizon in a lavish blue. Everything was beautifully polished, the blocks of private flats, the public buildings, the fashion stores, the restaurants as well as the gardens where children played like little angels. Such a sight made you acutely aware of your imperfections. You felt old and ugly.

An imposing flight of steps led up to the Opera spread out on a platform, silhouetted against the sky like a jewel in its open casket. I had never seen anything quite like it except perhaps the Taj Mahal. Both buildings were situated poles apart, one an ode to death, the other a hymn to life. Feeling out of place, I urged Richard to return to the safety of our hotel.

Our friend Régine Cuzin, curator of the overseas exhibitions at Paris City Hall, wreathed with flaming red hair, matching the surroundings, was waiting for us in the dining room. Waiters dressed as Mephistopheles were busy in the restaurant.

Régine burst out laughing when I told her my impressions. 'As Richard says, I think you must be carried away by your imagination as a novelist,' she joked. 'Sydney is a very pretty town, I agree, but I've never seen any age discrimination or cult of the body beautiful.'

The following morning, at eight o'clock, we climbed on board one of the numerous ferries which crossed the bay bound for Manly, a resort Régine had keenly recommended. In that little town, cooked over and over again by the sun, reigned the same atmosphere of unbridled beauty. Handsome young men in coloured wetsuits were surfing while on the beach of white sand a tangle of bodies was lined up in harmony. We lunched on a terrace surrounded by young girls in bikinis showing an abundance of tanned skin whereas the boys were paradoxically encased in tracksuits. Although it was their winter, the weather was fairly warm. We walked into a tourist shop that sold art and aboriginal crafts.

The manager was trying to sell a musical instrument to a couple of reluctant Americans. 'It's a didgeridoo,' he explained, manipulating a long wooden cylinder. 'All you have to do is blow here.'

We ended up relaxing on deck chairs by the sea while the sun dipped behind the horizon.

After such a delightful day, the evening at the French Cultural Centre was a disappointment. Ilena, the organizer, although charming and welcoming, had made no attempt at publicity and a handful of spectators sat adrift in a room decorated with inevitable views of the Eiffel Tower, the viaduct at Millau and the Mont Saint-Michel. I bravely began to speak and for almost an hour managed to conduct a languid discussion about my work. Miraculously, in the tiny audience was a guy from Martinique, the only person who had heard of me. He quickly stood up to shake my hand. 'What a pity so few people came. I've read all your books and I know a lot of teachers at the university who would have come to listen to you.'

His name was Gérard La Cascade and he managed a travel agency. He had left Martinique on an impulse while earning a comfortable living selling spectacle frames to short-sighted pupils from the Lycée Schoelcher.

He offered to show us around the next day since he owned a car.

'We'll go to Bondi Beach,' he promised. 'It's the surfing centre of the world.'

The French cultural services took us for dinner to a restaurant a few miles outside Sydney. Going down a stone staircase, you arrived onto an immense terrace overlooking the sea. Lights were twinkling on the other side of the bay.

'It's a seafood restaurant,' Ilena told us. 'In Australia, the seafood is the best in the world. I expect you like oysters?'

My answer in the negative resulted in silence—and everyone looked at me in horror. What had I dared say? The French cultural services, even the ambassadors, have always greeted me with the utmost courtesy despite being fully aware of my political opinions, of my belief in independence for Guadeloupe and my being a member of the UPLG movement. But to openly declare that I didn't like oysters was an unheard of scandal. I have no idea why! Fortunately, the wine broke the ice and I chose a grilled barramundi, a fish I had taken a liking to.

The next day, we met up with Gérard la Cascade and began our spin in the car.

'Don't be misled by this exceptional setting. It's not the Caribbean sea, warm and embracing. There are hidden dangers in this ocean, snakes several metres long, jellyfish, poisonous fish. There's no counting the number of foolhardy who've been swallowed up or had an arm or leg amputated by the sharks.'

He took us for lunch to the Fou-Fou Phalle Vert, managed by Lucas, another Martinican. Well, Martinican by name only! His mother, Anne, was a native of Melbourne. She had taken advantage of a study trip to Paris to be seduced by a law student from Martinique. When she announced she was pregnant, he told her he was married and a model father and refused to help. Lucas, therefore, had been raised to hate the Antilles, islands of seducers. Despite everything, Anne had been unable to get the myth of Martinique out of her son's head, and so, as soon as he was old enough, he went and spent three years on the island. Doing what? He never said.

The Fou-Fou Phalle Vert enjoyed an exceptional location. To the left was a seaside graveyard that would have done credit to Paul Valéry. Seabirds muffled up in their white plumage alighted on the tombs between which processions of mourners wound their way. Obviously, there was nothing traditional about the cuisine and Adélia would have had a thousand reasons to frown.

Yet while downing a saffron-coloured sea-urchin blaff, which was a blaff by name only, I was gripped by a violent emotion. Here we were, three Antilleans so far from our native islands, land of volcanoes and sugarcane, endeavouring to survive and give meaning to our lives. My eyes inexplicably brimmed with tears and I had to turn away to hide my face from Richard.

Back at the hotel we bumped into Ilena. She obviously wanted to be compensate for the failed cultural evening by giving us the wonderful surprise of two tickets for the opera the following evening.

'It's Verdi's *Nabucco*,' she said. 'It's an exceptional performance, transposed to modern times, to the land of Saddam Hussein. I myself haven't seen it yet.'

I couldn't find words to thank her enough. Lucky are those who are able to find their bearings around the mysteries of an opera and decipher those melodramatic and convoluted plots such as that of *Nabucco*. As for the transposition to Saddam Hussein's Iraq— I was at a loss. At one point I saw a bearded, dark-skinned singer emerge from an underground cave. It was probably Saddam Hussein. Who knows?

There were a number of other reasons for an unforgettable evening. Richard and I sat down for dinner in the restaurant at the Opera. It was hung with black crepe like the inside of a catafalque. Waiters dressed in long black tunics, their heads oddly wrapped in white turbans, seemed to match their movements to the rhythm of the strange music in the background. I later learnt that the decor had been designed along the lines of the concert hall which was plunged in darkness except for the stage which emerged brilliantly lit. On hearing the first notes, I was overcome by the magical sounds and the powerful choir of Hebrew slaves. A remarkable direction shaped every movement of the actors and the choir. I got the impression of dying, being born again and starting a new life.

Paraphrasing Gaston Kelman whose book *I'm Black but I Don't Like Cassava* was a bestseller, I could well say that as a Guadeloupean I don't like the traditional music of the *gwo ka*. Very early on, however, I discovered opera. One day, Jeanne-Marie, a university friend of mine who ended up as a nun among the lepers in Africa, took me under her wing and accompanied me to Chantecler, a record shop on the boulevard Saint-Michel, to get me to hear 'real music'. She had me listen to Mozart's *Magic Flute*— and I was transported. This love for opera, which I have kept all these years, was not instilled in me by my family and its somewhat mediocre musical tastes. My parents owned a gramophone, and, in order to occupy the long evenings at Sarcelles, we would listen tirelessly to the Barcarolle from *The Tales of Hoffman*, *The Violin Player from Cremona* and Gounod's *Ave Maria*. When he had one too many glasses of rum, my father would strike up an old barrack-room song until my mother made him shut up. My father had led a dissolute life during his first marriage, cheating on his wife and drinking far too much. Bewitched by my mother's beauty, he had married her, little foreseeing she would make him live a life as regular as clockwork.

My mother herself had quite a pretty high-strung voice and constantly sang sentimental ballads in French and Creole. I can still quote the lyrics of her favourite song:

Oh, never fall in love, never fall in love. When love vanishes all that is left are flowers. I took my heart and gave it to an ingrate, a heartless young man devoid of love.

The day before we left, a journalist interviewed me over the phone about the Melbourne Book Festival.

'The Melbourne Book Festival?' I repeated.

'Haven't you heard of it?' he exclaimed. 'It's the biggest book fair in Australia. There's a large focus on books written in French.'

Unfortunately, it was too late to change my plans.

That visit to Australia has left me with the bitter feeling of something unfinished, a missed opportunity. Apart from the beauty of the country, I learnt little about its cultural riches. However much I read the books by Australian writers, attend the Australian film screenings in New York, I cannot change this impression. When I heard that Peter Carey taught in New York, I thought about sending him an email.

But I could never get round to doing so. What would I say? That kind of advance was contrary to my nature and my habit. If I were ten years younger, I would have gone back to Sydney, at my expense if need be, but every day I withdrew into myself and it seemed more and more unlikely. Looking back, I realize that Australia had signified something I had been unable to decipher.

These visits on the double to countries whose cuisine, and consequently their culture, I boasted of mastering were not to last much longer. I had travelled a good deal of the planet. To the countries I have mentioned we should add Indonesia, Hong Kong, part of China, Ecuador, Mexico, Peru, Chile, not to mention sub-Saharan Africa. What was I left with? Magnificent pictures that were gradually fading and turning to sepia. My life was about to change and I didn't know it.

A few years previously, during one of those lunches for the press that Simone Gallimard was fond of giving, a well-known writer asked me what I was looking for on hearing me describe my numerous travels.

I have been asked such a question on several occasions. During an imaginary conversation with Victoire my grandmother, she blamed me for neglecting to write a novel about her. In fact, what was I looking for? I suddenly began to take a liking to a settled way of life.

I realized that New York whose vitality and highly charged character I had liked so much was also a tender, protective city. The buses kneeled to enable the disabled like myself to enter. Benches arranged along the frenzied streets allowed those tired of walking to rest. I gradually began to build up a new relationship with my surroundings. As a result, I took a liking to the street fairs along Broadway that I had once despised. I lived on Riverside Drive, a short walk away. You could find anything for sale, hand-knitted turtleneck pullovers, tri-coloured scarves, Peruvian bonnets, bold patterned socks, loads of which I bought for my grandchildren. Red-nosed clowns vied with jugglers. Elsewhere, a crowd of children sat quietly on the ground listening to the storytellers and musicians.

I discovered that you don't have to travel to a country to get to know its cuisine, something I had always thought fundamental. At a Turkish food stand at one of these street fairs, I tasted for the first time imam bayildi, a dish made of eggplant and tomatoes slowly cooked in the oven. At a Greek stand I sampled stuffed squid and lined up for my slice of Peruvian chicken cooked in beer.

Likewise, the atmosphere at the dinners I made for my friends discreetly changed. They became less ostentatious. I no longer showed off my recipes. I learnt to serve conviviality.

Yet in the midst of all these transformations I kept a dream deep down in my heart. Although I had resigned myself to never being integrated into the African American community, I never stopped regretting that there was so little contact between us. Whenever I passed the black professors from the African American Studies Department or the English Department, we would exchange cordial smiles and warm 'Hi's', but that's as far as it went. Although my classes were a rite of passage for students from the Caribbean, North Africa and sub-Saharan Africa, no African American student registered. They obviously preferred James Baldwin, Ralph Ellison and especially Toni Morrison to Aimé Césaire, Edouard Glissant and Sony Labou Tansi. My editor for my books in English was an African American. I had invited her several times to dinner with the hope of getting to know her better. But she remained elusive.

You can understand therefore that I was overjoyed when a certain Debra Harrison asked me to join her annual creative-writing workshop. It had been created in 1960, she proudly emphasized, and had hosted some of the most prestigious African American writers. She lived in Macomb, a small town in Georgia. I had great difficulty persuading Richard that my presence in that godforsaken place was indispensable. Unconvinced, he went off to see his mother whose health was deteriorating.

The small town of Macomb was founded at the start of the nineteenth century by a group of slaves whose master, Jonathan Cape Middlewood, had freed them while on his deathbed. The group was composed of six women, all coffee-coloured illegitimate children of Middlewood, their male companions and twenty or so children. In order to avoid the frequent raids at that time, Macomb had been built on top of a hill; later, it moved down to the plain. So there were now two Macombs: Upper Macomb, still known as Old Macomb; and Lower Macomb, mainly inhabited by farm employees working in the surrounding orchards with their families. Upper Macomb consisted of a main street intersected by half a dozen side streets. The focal point was without doubt not the church or town hall but Debra's house, a spacious wooden building with a dozen rooms dating back to the nineteenth century. Debra was a corpulent woman but surprisingly nimble. Her face had lovely, regular features and it was a pity she had let her body become so fat.

When I stepped off the bus from Atlanta, she grasped me with both hands. 'It's really you! I must be dreaming!'

Surprised by her expression of bliss, I asked which of my books she had read.

'*Segu*,' she articulated unctuously. 'I can't tell you how many times I have read it. It's a masterpiece.'

Thereupon she turned to a group of young people probably waiting for the next Greyhound bus and declared: 'This is one of the world's greatest writers. She has done us the honour of coming to see us.'

The young people didn't seem overly moved by such a declaration but I, on the contrary, was stupefied by the extravagance of her words. Don't misunderstand me—I am not in the least sensitive to flattery. In fact, I believe that the flatterer doubts my intellectual capacities and is making fun of me. But here I was prepared to swallow it all, hook line and sinker, since Debra was my last chance, the chance I had been waiting for all these years, to make my entrance in a world that had always evaded me.

She grabbed my suitcase and headed for the exit. I had trouble keeping up with her since the road was a steep climb. Realizing it, she held out a helping hand. 'You have difficulty walking?' she asked. 'I'll massage you with essential oils. All the teachers are here now. Marita Gonzalez and Amy Montrose arrived this morning. You're familiar with these novelists, aren't you?'

I had never heard of them.

'Only Laura Adamson is missing,' she continued. 'She's driving down from New Haven.'

'Laura Adamson!' I cried. 'What a coincidence! We were invited the same year to the Calabash Festival in Jamaica.'

'She's an extraordinary woman and so talented. You know that she is rumoured to be next year's poet laureate?'

Debra's home, where the four workshop teachers were housed, was an elegant building. The pediment on its facade bore the slightly pretentious name The Zora Neale Hurston Study and Reflection Center. The forty or so students were housed on the other side of the street, in a hotel called The New Negro after the title of Alan Locke's famous essay.

I know there are many ways in which I could describe this stay in Macomb. I could make fun of Debra's constant hyperboles: 'The teachers I've invited are among some of the world's most famous writers.' 'The students come from all over America and are extremely gifted and intelligent.' 'This work-shop is rewarding beyond imagination.'

I could poke fun at the fanatical intellectualism of the nightly entertainments. On the first evening there was a concert of atonal, obtuse and enigmatic music. On the second, a ballet where the dancers interpreted in an incomprehensible fashion an even-more-incomprehensible African American novel. On the third, an esoteric poetry recital.

I could cast doubt on Debra's affirmations. Had she really been head of the African American Studies Department at the famous Morehouse College in Atlanta? Had she really been the partner of one of the NAACP's important members, now deceased, who had given the Center a solid endowment before he died? Had she really played a decisive role in the civil rights movement? Had she really been so close to the Black Panthers that she was arrested and spent long weeks in prison? Was she really the living example of an African American militant? The famous writers who adorned the walls of the dining room, had they really been interested in the Zora Neal Hurston Study and Reflection Center? And wasn't it outrageous that Debra lived with Willard, a poet with an inspired look, twenty years younger and 40 kilos thinner, whom you never knew whether he was a student or a teacher since he constantly switched from one to the other?

I could poke fun at this stay. Instead, I prefer to broach it as a total immersion, like landing on a planet belonging to another solar system.

Every morning at seven on the dot, Debra would come into my bedroom and massage me with an oil of everlasting flower whose peppery scent I can still smell. She hadn't yet slipped on the stylish habit of an intellectual; she was still a woman, like the rest of us, even motherly. Her hands were like fleshy paws and very soft. My blood flowed warm and energized under their pressure. She did not give me the political and militant lectures she reserved for the students, but conversed in an intimate manner. She told me about her mother who died when she was ten; about her sisters who lived in Atlanta with their families and had become strangers; about her brothers who had emigrated to Canada and whom she no longer heard from. Perhaps they were all the fruit of her imagination. Nevertheless, they touched my heart. I too lost my mother when I was very young. I too had little contact with my brothers and sisters.

At eight o'clock, breakfast brought us all together in the dining room whose walls were covered with writers' photos and quotations. Though some of the citations were pretty feeble. A certain C. Wilson declared, for example: 'Life is a road furrowed with ruts. Let us learn how to avoid them.'

I dug into the grits, ham and honeyed chicken sausage. I discovered to my delight the fried green tomatoes from Georgia.

Classes began sharp at nine. The students were far from idle: they attended two creative- writing workshops on the novel, one on poetry and another on theatre. Debra had not exaggerated when she said they came from far afield: some had come from California, some from Washington, some even Hawaii. They had often managed to publish their first novel or collection of poetry but with little success. The immense respect they showed for the teachers practically ruined any discussion. They all began their comments with: 'If I may, Professor Condé, dare I say that . . . .' Thus my seminars at Macomb lacked the familiarity, even intimacy, which was characteristic of my classes at Columbia.

Those who took part in my workshop professed a deep admiration for *Segu*. They claimed it was listed on many of the black secondary schools' curricula. I couldn't believe my ears. I wondered whether they were telling the truth and hadn't been duly coached by Debra. Gradually, however, I ended up believing them, telling myself that the author and her text lead two very distinct, even antagonistic, lives. I who lamented of going unrecognized, even excluded, from African American literature, was being told that *Segu* had here contributed in its own small way to the construction of the black psyche. As a result, I rediscovered the book I had almost forgotten. I realized the value it held for black Americans, constantly confronted with racism. This depiction of a proud, noble Africa before its decadence, the result of the slave trade and colonization, was a reassuring factor in their eyes. I did not have this in mind when I wrote it, but doesn't a book turn out to be what a reader wants it to be?

At noon, teachers and students crossed the street to lunch at the New Negro, the hotel managed by Nikki, a relative of Debra. She was just as voluminous but legally married to an austere sixty-year-old who was the Center's handyman. We lunched in the Emmett Till Dining Room under the eyes of Martin Luther King Jr, Coretta and their young children. Nikki was a true chef. Her speciality was braised chicken with chanterelles, quail fricassee and caramelized pork with peaches. But when I dared enquire about her recipes, she adamantly refused to tell me.

'Literature is the same as cooking,' Debra said, laughing at my vexed expression. 'Beware of plagiarism.'

'Not true!' I shouted. 'There's no plagiarism in cooking!'

The afternoon was Willard's moment of glory. Everyone piled into the Rosa Parks Room, its doors and windows closed and its curtains drawn to keep out the light. Willard chose two or three films from the large collection of authors' interviews and documentaries owned by the Center. Nothing was missing, from Richard Wright seated massively at a table in a cafe on the rue Tournon in Paris and boasting of the benefits of Communism to Romare Bearden dressed in a flowery shirt in Saint-Martin explaining the correspondences between the blues and painting to Amiri Baraka raging as usual against the white world. Willard would comment on their arguments and Debra would respond, a dialogue faltering between esotericism and the ridiculous.

'What is art?' Willard would ask grandiloquently.

'A dot on the *i* of life,' Debra would answer.

Apparently I was the only one smothering giggles.

Sometimes these exchanges lasted so long that night fell before they were over. Dinner however was better, more relaxed. Nikki cooked a barbecue in the hotel courtyard and the aroma of grilled meat floated up to the sky like an offering. The students loosened up, laughed and chattered. Some even dared go down to the liquor store in Lower Macomb to buy beer. Unfortunately, the cultural evenings strained the atmosphere again.

It was then that my relations with Laura Adamson took an unexpected turn, and I became extremely close to this woman who years earlier I hadn't much cared for. Lying side by side like two schoolgirls, we would chat until the early hours of the morning. Up till then, I had never confided in another woman. I was never very close to my sisters who were too old to take an interest in me; and the fear of boring my few girlfriends prevented me from letting off steam in their company. Suddenly, I discovered how blissful it was to talk about oneself openly and unaffectedly. Like me, Laura had suffered a lot when she was younger. At twenty-two, she and her two children had been abandoned by her husband, a rich Jewish lawyer. Convinced she had committed an unpardonable sin by marrying a white man, she had remarried a black militant who gave her two more children. When she caught him trying to seduce her younger sister, she divorced him. Ever since, she kept both white and black men at bay. I tried to console her. I told her that in spite of four children and forty years of bad luck, I had ended up finding happiness.

'I'm not surprised,' she told me. 'Nothing can shake your spirits. You are so strong, so sure of yourself.'

Sure of myself? How could she be so mistaken, I who am scared of everything? I attempted to explain:

'No, I'm not strong. But I've always kept deep down in me the conviction that I would make it.'

Laura made no secret of her reservations about the Center and Debra.

'I came,' she said, 'because I've been invited at least ten times. But I was warned. Debra forces a straitjacket onto every student with the names of James Baldwin, August Wilson or Rita Dove. There's no room for creativity. Do you remember the wonderful spontaneity at the Calabash Festival?'

I had to confess that I had made several criticisms of that 'wonderful spontaneity'.

'A craftsman who wants to make a table goes to find a skilled cabinet maker,' I answered. 'He has to respect certain rules. Why should it be any different in literature?'

We never managed to agree. But I did make her leap up when I suggested the Center should open up to Indian, Chinese, Japanese or even Western writers.

'To white folks, you mean?' Laura exclaimed, horrified.

'In literature, there are neither whites nor blacks. Literature is colour blind.'

'Oh, come on! In order to write, you have to know where you come from.'

Around one in the morning, Laura and I tiptoed down to the kitchen where she concocted a herb tea scented with cinnamon.

'It warms the body and helps you sleep,' she said.

We sipped our tea next to the window wide open onto the darkness and surprising silence of the night. It was as if the town lay under a lid of lead. No distant call of drums drifted on the air, no hum of human voices, no rustling of insects amid the foliage.

The thought of Richard alone by his mother's bedside filled me with anguish and remorse. Had I at least found what I had come to look for at the Center? But what had I come to look for? I could no longer see the situation clearly, and deep down felt at a loss.

The closing Saturday was deadly dull. As early as nine in the morning, some important-looking men arrived from Atlanta, then two NAACP officials from Baltimore, genuine caricatures smoking cigars and wearing heavy double-breasted suits. They filled the New Negro hotel's dining room as they joined us for coffee. Their luxury limousines parked in front of the hotel gave the impression that culture was indeed a great asset. Then came a series of speeches each more pretentious than the other, on hackneyed subjects such as: 'The pen is mightier than the sword', 'Without culture an individual languishes and dies', 'Culture should be listed as one of the basic needs defined by UNESCO'.

The most painful part of the morning was the never-ending graduation ceremony, carried out by Debra in a scarlet toga which accentuated her figure even more. Each student received a homily, bristling with superlatives. Suddenly I couldn't take it any longer. I'd had my fill of exaggerations and amphigoric speeches. I couldn't even touch the typical meal of the Old South prepared by Nikki: a slightly salted pork stew garnished with chestnut puree and boiled sweet potatoes. I jumped into Macomb's sole rental car and drove to Atlanta to take the flight back to New York. There, my life was waiting for me. I was overjoyed to reunite with my husband, my students and the simplicity of my daily routine. For two weeks I had slipped on borrowed clothes that had been too tight under the arms. Now, at last, I was free and anonymous again.

One or two months later I got a big surprise. Medgar Evers College informed me that I had been awarded the Toni Morrison Prize for my outstanding contribution to literature. Me! I saw the hand of Debra at work. How could I show her my gratitude? Thanks to her, I was officially invited to sit at the masters' table. You'll better understand my feelings once you know what Medgar Evers College stands for in the African American community. It's a kind of pantheon. Located at the heart of Brooklyn, it proudly bears the name of a martyr in the fight for freedom— Evers was assassinated in 1963 by a member of the Ku Klux Klan. In *The Story of the Cannibal Woman*, I recount how my pride quickly changed into disappointment. My prize was given by a professor who mispronounced my name. Since I was the last to be

honoured, at the end of the ceremony, the amphitheatre was half empty, littered with paper cups and
trash. I was convinced that the few people present
did not understand a word of my thank-you speech
because of my French accent. Unlike Rosélie, the
heroine in my novel, there wasn't even the consolation of an Anthony Turley to flirt with.

What became of my friendship with Laura
Adamson? Following our reunion in Macomb, we
saw each other frequently. She spent weekends in
New York at one of her aunts' or cousins' which
allowed her to have dinner with us at Riverside
Drive. Her gentle, tolerant mood went down well in
the company of our friends. She only breathed fire
and fury if we dared criticize Barack Obama whom
she hero-worshipped. She who thought nothing of
ordering from Pizza Hut poked fun at my cooking
sprees. 'What are you trying to prove? That you're
not a true intellectual?'

'What do you mean? I cook because I like cooking. That's all.'

'You know that things are not as simple as that.
Cooking for you is a form of resistance.'

Resistance to what? To this conformist world
where I was sinking in spite of myself? In August, she
suddenly announced that she was leaving for the university in Entebbe where she had been offered the
job of heading the English Department. Entebbe? In
that godforsaken place, she would constantly come
up against the memory of Idi Amin's crimes whose

memory had recently been revived by a successful film.

'My children no longer need me,' she explained. 'My youngest son has just been admitted to Dartmouth.'

Beneath those rational words I thought I could detect a kind of suicide, a renunciation of a life that had not fulfilled its promise. But however hard I tried, I never managed to get her to change her plans. She left in September. Our relations were reduced to sporadic emails.

ADIEU FOULARD, ADIEU MADRAS

After over a year of procrastinating and hesitating, Richard and I had to come to grips with the dire decision to sell our house in Montebello and buy an apartment in Paris. My health was not getting any better. Travelling between New York and Guadeloupe was exhausting me a little more every year. Moreover, we were both of the opinion that it would be better to live in a city where access to health care was easier. Guadeloupe is not lacking in excellent doctors but they are always snowed under with work. To get an appointment is an exploit in itself. In a certain respect, this departure might seem like a painful ending. Some twenty years earlier, we had joyfully abandoned Europe for the French Antilles. Richard was bored with his job as a translator. As for me, I have already said that this return to the native land not only coincided with my second marriage but also symbolized the advent of a new life. *Heremakhonon* was a premonitory sign. I was finally going to get to know happiness.

In order to track down the house of our dreams, we scoured the island from north to south and east to west. We looked longingly at an apartment with a balcony overlooking the beach at Deshaies. We fell for a sumptuous villa in Le Moule. Finally, we were won over by a traditional change-of-air house in Montebello. I've already said how I liked the region of Petit Bourg. For someone who passes through absent-mindedly it's not worth the detour. But for me it brings back so many memories. It was in Sarcelles, a few kilometres further on, where I spent my holidays with my parents. As I said in *Tales from the Heart*, my father would play the gentleman farmer. He would slip on his rough khaki-coloured clothes, put on his pith helmet, and, taking me by the hand, show me how to feel the weight of the cocoa pods.

But we quickly realized that the purchase of the house in Montebello was not a good deal. Far from it. We had no idea of the amount of work it needed. At the first strike of the pickaxe the walls collapsed, and all that was left was the roof joggling comically over the attic. Our architect needed over a year's work to put it all back to life again.

Yet Montebello remains full of unforgettable memories.

When we at last took possession of the house, we designed the garden ourselves. My first task was to plant an ylang-ylang, a fetish tree that had filled my childhood with its scent. When I was a little girl, I used to macerate its flowers in alcohol and make a lotion with a heady perfume which I would spray over my dolls. I also planted a traveller's tree in the middle of the lawn. And a hedge of poinciana with yellow and red flowers and beds of hibiscus. And ginger lilies because my mother loved them.

Oddly enough, taking leave of Guadeloupe did not affect me deep down. I knew I was taking the island with me, that it would always be with me wherever I went. Going back to the places I was fond of was not to say farewell; rather, it was to capture a final picture in my heart that would be closer to reality.

I began by crossing that rough stretch of sea that led to the island of Marie-Galante. A few years earlier, a small troop of faithful mourners had accompanied my friend and mentor, Guy Tirolien, to his grave. The following year, I added regional literature to my seminar at Columbia and taught three Guadeloupean writers I admired: Sony Rupaire, Max Rippon and Guy Tirolien.

Fortunately, Michelle was still there, still as tall as she was wide. Exhausted from having raised eleven children, she had sold her restaurant, The Hungry Clam. Reluctant to leave her pots and pans entirely, she filled in on Sundays for the cook at a hotel that had just opened on the beach at Saint-Louis.

She was wildly opposed to our idea of leaving. 'You're leaving for health reasons? I'll put you back on your feet,' she proclaimed. 'Trust me!'

Consequently, she entrusted me to Norbert a sort of obeah man, related to her husband Paco. An old black man as thin and bony as a guava twig, he had me lie down on a wooden plank and hammered my body with the edge of his hard, calloused hand. It was agony. I went to sleep exhausted but woke up feeling better. The relief, however, did not last very long: a day or two at most.

Michelle and I rivalled each other with recipes while Paco and Richard downed enough goblets of Père Labat rum to knock you senseless. One evening, Michelle had us taste a fressure, a dish nobody cooks any longer, composed of pig offal spiced and grilled on a barbecue. I had to acknowledge Michelle had outdone me.

When it came to saying goodbye, we hugged each other and wept like we used to as children, when Adélia's and my mother's nimble hands striped our backsides.

Michelle couldn't stop scolding me. 'You're too impatient. I'd have taken you to all the obeahmen and you would have ended up well and truly cured.'

Then it was Northern Grande Terre's turn. I went for a last meal to the Château des Feuilles which we frequented since it had a pool. Raky, Leila's daughter, who always spent the summer holidays with us, learnt swimming there. The food was good but not special. What inspired me was the surrounding expanse of a barren, stony landscape. Not far from there was the Gate of Hell, pounded by the furious waves of the Atlantic Ocean. The violet-coloured sea was always in a fit of rage. When I wrote *Windward Heights*, an adaptation of Emily Brontë's masterpiece

Wuthering Heights, it was amid this austere decor that I situated the house L'Engoulevent in which Cathy and Razié lived, the latter being my Guadeloupean version of Heathcliff.

I'll take time here to relate the mixed fate of that novel. It was totally ignored in France except for a negative review in some obscure magazine. In England, it enjoyed a varied fortune. The Emily Brontë Society was outraged and dealt the book a fatal blow with the words 'shocking' and 'worthless'. On the other hand, in a bookstore in Canterbury, it was nominated the booksellers' choice which got my mother-in-law very excited. Alas, when she enquired about sales she was told not a single copy had been sold. The United States, however, gave it a warm reception and I was swamped with letters from enthusiastic readers. It is now studied in the English departments of many universities.

We then crossed the island to Anse à la Barque on the Leeward shore. When I was barely ten, it was here that the beauty of nature first made a deep impression on me. I had gone to spend the weekend with my brother at Basse-Terre, as I did once a month. Since he was my godfather, I recall, my parents insisted on preserving a pretence of close relations between us. My brother obeyed them. He had me sit in the back of his car and we drove around the southern tip of Guadeloupe: Saint-Claude, Matouba, Deshaies and Vieux-Habitants. That particular weekend he was accompanied by the mulatto woman he was soon to marry. I was intimidated by that young woman with white skin and green eyes, so different from those we usually kept company with.

She started up a conversation: 'I hear you're doing well at school,' she said. 'Especially in French.'

'Yes,' I stammered.

'What do you want to be when you grow up?'

'Nurse,' I let out.

I said that quite out of the blue, because it was the first job that came to mind.

'Nurse?' she exclaimed with contempt. 'No need to pass your baccalaureate and be first in every class to become a nurse!'

Fortunately, we had arrived at our destination. The Citroën turned onto a rough road and jolted down to the sea. Suddenly, the splendour of the landscape made my heart race.

The place had changed quite a bit. It was marred by a number of cheap, ugly restaurants. Richard and I chose the one that seemed to be the most original, a straw beach hut overshadowed by a large portrait of Commandant Cousteau, a frequent visitor to the region. A few kilometres away was the marine reserve named after him. I remember that lunch was terrible but that the fruit punch was excellent.

Then I made my way to La Rose, not far from Montebello. I once knew it as a place bustling with excitement. It was the site of a rum distillery which belonged to friends of my parents, M. and Mme Bolivar. Their white house with blue shutters stood at the top of a hill and overlooked the surrounding countryside. We would sit on the wrap-around gallery and Alix Bolivar would have us taste an aged rum of which he was very proud.

'It's as good as the ones from Martinique,' he said. 'All it needs is its label of origin. But we Guadeloupeans have never known how to promote ourselves.'

A path wound down to the river. A large pool curved under the arch of rose apple trees which gave their name to the place. Children chased each other into the water, splashing as they went, while others dived off the bank. Young Apollos showed off their muscles and other attributes. The washerwomen sang at the top of their voices as they spread their sheets and towels over the rocks; some of them beat their washing with great slaps. Dressed in Petit Bateau panties, I practised my swimming guided by Sandrino. Alas, the distillery went bankrupt in the 1980s. Monsieur and Madame died. The dismal launderettes killed off the washerwomen. Doctors discovered bilharzias in the water and put a stop to bathing. Finally, the Conseil Général moved the road, as at my parents' place in Sarcelles, and La Rose was left abandoned, overrun with aquatic weeds.

My last place of pilgrimage was to the island of La Désirade. Marianne Bosshard, whom we met while she was teaching at the Naval Academy in Annapolis near Washington DC, had retired to the island and lived in a small concrete house not far from the lepers' graveyard. While researching the island's archives, she discovered that the Boucolons, the name of my father's family, were originally from Grande Anse. Once freed and given a civil status, they had decided to settle near Petit Bourg on the mainland of Guadeloupe. I was deeply moved when I learnt of this unknown part of my history. My visits to the small island became more frequent and I even dedicated a novel to it: *Desirada*, the name Christopher Columbus' sailors gave it on its first sighting.

The rumour of our departure soon spread like a rock thrown into a pond. José, whose visits to Montebello were far and few between, suddenly arrived at lunch in the company of two other patriots. 'Your leaving Guadeloupe is nothing short of treason,' he proclaimed. 'You're abandoning us whereas the fight is far from over.'

I shrugged and said sadly: 'What fight are you talking about? Nobody is interested in independence except for a group of sixty-year-olds like us.'

'What on earth are you saying?' he fumed. 'Independence is on everyone's mind. It's a dream that is taking its time, that's all. That's why the young have lost patience and turned to drugs and violence.'

I realized the discussion was going nowhere and murmured: 'The reason I'm leaving, José, is because of my health.'

This had little effect.

'Precisely, it's here you would have found the best obeah man who would have put you back on your feet in next to no time. And won't you miss the climate?'

My old friend Eddie thought likewise. 'You prefer the winters in Paris and especially New York to the godgiven climate of Guadeloupe, its sun and its sea?'

How could I explain that I was not really leaving? Sitting in Riverside Park, surrounded by children sledding down the snowy slopes, I knew that if I closed my eyes I would see always the shining sun of the tropics.

During those final weeks I carefully noted in a large book the recipes I might well forget: a stew of root vegetables; a breadfruit soufflé; a saltfish mix; and a gratin of green ambarella fruit.

Prompted by a bundle of political-sentimental reasons, rather stupid I admit, I was intent on selling Montebello solely to Guadeloupeans. I didn't take into account the law of the market. Built with traditional, plain angelica wood, our house was far from the flashy, modern constructions in concrete. Moreover, it required constant maintenance against termites and the weather. As a result, although numerous Guadeloupeans filed through to visit, none put in a bid. In the end, we had to sell to a French couple. They were especially delighted by the little house we had built in the garden where the African American poet Quincy Troupe and his wife

Margaret had once stayed. They were going to do it up for their two teenage sons.

Our departure was filled with omens. Lightning struck a mango tree in the garden and split it in two. Yet there was no storm that night. As a result of technical problems on one of their planes, Air France changed our flight to 14 July. What Bastille was I going to tear down? The day before we left, Richard fell and broke his wrist. A symbolic fracture which we were told meant separation. He made a terrible journey numbed by painkillers and his arm in a temporary sling, and the express recommendation to go immediately to the Saint-Antoine hospital on his arrival in Paris. Later, when we could laugh about it, he told me that while he was shivering with pain the nurses from Guadeloupe whispered to the surgeon: 'It's Maryse Condé's husband.'

Barely interested because he had never heard the name before, the surgeon politely nodded.

Neither Richard nor I were particularly pleased to be back in Paris. As usual, Paris looked down at me, cold and aloof, and treated me like a stranger. Nevertheless, certain places retained their magic. We went for dinner to Brasserie Bofinger where we used to be frequent customers. I liked the place, the gold and the gilt, the elegance of the waiters and the solemn way they shouldered the dishes as if they were priests handing out the sacrament. What saddened me was having to ask for a table downstairs for I could no longer climb to the floor above. It was a premonition of what I was to become. Fortunately, our neighbours were a friendly couple of Americans seated in front of an enormous seafood platter. They talked to us about Paris with that passion only Americans feel for France. For Americans, France is not a colonial power and my friends have never understood my claims for independence. They cannot understand that the French language which I speak so well can be considered an imposition. In short, in their eyes, I should be extremely proud to be an adoptive daughter.

We began looking for an apartment, and, after weeks of searching, we finally found a suitable match. We became friends with M. and Mme Bert who planned to sell us their apartment on the rue Chapon in the Marais district. They were the ones who told us about the Taxi Jaune and Otis Lebert. The restaurant looked like an informal dining room where customers and habitués felt at home. The atmosphere was lively and relaxed. Around forty customers settled in to enjoy themselves and loudly decipher the menu chalked up on a slate hung on the wall. Nothing exotic at the Taxi Jaune. At a time when Asian cuisine was in fusion just about everywhere, Otis kept to French cooking: delightfully traditional, seasonal vegetables, country flavours. Oddly enough, these rigid standards appealed to me after having roamed the globe.

In December, we flew back to New York. I was free to do as I please since I had retired from teaching at Columbia. I hadn't even kept my office hours for that would mean climbing up 116th Street twice a week to the university. With the help of Richard, I would only go on campus for a lecture or a conference.

That's how I got to listen to Claude Lanzmann, Alice Kaplan, Edwidge Danticat and especially a dear friend of mine whom I hadn't seen for years, Aminata Sow Fall from Senegal. Seeing her immediately brought back all my younger years when I had only just written *Heremakhonon* and I was a lecturer at Nanterre University. Lilyan Kesteloot had insisted I attend a conference at the university in Dakar. I was on my own. At that time, in order to break up the routine of marriage, Richard and I didn't hesitate to go our separate ways for a few days, even a week. I was not used to being in the company of intellectual women from Africa and was envious of Mme Ki-Zerbo, Angélique Savané and Fatou Gueye. I was especially struck by Aminata, dressed in an elegant embroidered boubou and an immense head dress. It was rumoured that her novel *The Beggars' Strike* might be awarded the Prix Goncourt.

She laughed about it. 'You must be joking!' she protested. 'If it were true, France would no longer be France.'

Despite our differences, we became friends. She invited me for dinner at her place. There were so many little girls and boys constantly coming up to me for a kiss on their cheeks that I couldn't help asking her how many children she had.

'You shouldn't ask,' she replied with her characteristic blend of brusqueness and humour. 'Children are God's gift—you accept them, but you don't count.'

The dinner served in the courtyard under the stars was magnificent. It consisted of a soupokandia, perhaps a little too rich, that I have never ventured to cook, comprising dried fish, yet (conch), seafood, smoked fish, meat and okra cooked in palm oil. It is garnished with rice and, since it is somewhat heavy, should be washed down abundantly with bissap, the national drink of Senegal made from hibiscus flowers.

Years later I returned to Dakar for the promotion of *Segu*. As I have already said, the book was the subject of a web of intrigue in the African countries where I presented it. The watchword went out to writers to boycott my presentations. In Dakar, Sembene Ousmane and Aminata Sow Fall were the only ones who refused to submit to this diktat. 'If they don't like your book,' Sembene said angrily, 'let them come and say so and explain why.'

'What are they blaming me for?' I murmured in dismay.

'For being a woman,' Aminata uttered violently. 'Well, we'll show them what we're capable of.'

She was the one who gave me the courage to defend myself.

Once her presentation was over, we all went up the first floor of La Maison Française at Columbia where American-style refreshments were being served: cheese cubes and white wine. But neither of us was interested in eating. We were satisfied discussing the memory of those years when we were capable of fighting everything and everyone.

I had time on my hands to write. I should have been overjoyed since I had always put off my writing in order to prepare and deliver my classes. But now, every morning, my students filed in and out of Riverside Drive, some requesting help with their theses, others asking for interviews or wanting letters of recommendation and others wishing to discuss subjects which they considered terribly important. But the afternoons belonged to me. I could have locked myself away, turned up the music and worked. Unfortunately, something was gnawing at me and making me sterile. After twenty books or so, wasn't I running the risk of repeating myself and rambling on about the same things? How could I innovate? Was I destined to repeat over and over the same stories, since my obsessions and preoccupations never varied? The world, however, was changing radically around me, and readers with it. I sat staring at my computer for hours but nothing came to inspire me. This lasted for days.

Suddenly, one afternoon, a face floated before my eyes. It belonged to Kassem Ramzi, a former student of mine, one of the most brilliant I have come across. He was born in Lebanon and described to me the hatred sparked by the world for Arabs and Muslims. Every time he took a plane, he was subjected to endless and humiliating checks. Now that he was a lawyer and defended the prisoners at Guantanamo, he was the object of mistrust by his white colleagues who claimed he could not be objective and sought to oust him. I had a flash of inspiration. That's what I should write about: such topics of a terrifying modernity. But they shouldn't be treated in a realistic fashion. I would intersperse my narrative with extravagant, even improbable, incidents. That's how I devised *Les Belles Ténébreuses* (The Dark Lovelies) which I first called *Les Pareurs de Mort* (The Terminators of Death). It's the story of two young men, professional embalmers, who maintain a strange relation with the corpses they are supposed to embellish for eternity.

Some two years later Ramzi read the book and didn't recognize himself.

'It's not my story,' he protested. 'It's pure invention.'

Yes, I confessed I had invented everything. But wasn't this fictional life better than his real life? Moreover, what imaginative life is not better than real life?

Travelling in My Dreams, Dreaming of Travelling

To say that my imposed sedentary life was a pain would be an understatement. The impression of help-lessness in the face of illness and old age was extremely distressing. The reason I didn't suffer as much as I expected was that for almost two years I discovered a defence mechanism, an unexpected anti-dote: I began to repeat certain travels in my dreams. I've always dreamt a lot and always sought to inter-pret my dreams. It's a tradition strongly rooted in Guadeloupe. In the lowliest of village shops, small brochures printed at the author's expense titled *The Key to Dreams* are on sale and claim to foresee the future thanks to past omens. I personally had been in the good hands of my mother who every morning had long conversations with her servants about her nocturnal adventures.

'I dreamt I was covered in blood,' she would lament.

'A good omen,' Julie reassured her. 'It means victory.'

Victory? What victory? Victory over whom, over what? I wondered as I sat silent in a corner of the bedroom. But my mother was obviously satisfied since she did not protest nor asked questions.

Some mornings my mother would sit glumly.

'I dreamt I was carrying a suitcase!'

'That's a bad omen,' Adélia claimed. 'It means illness.'

I listened very carefully, and, as early as ten, I was able to fabricate my own version of *The Key to Dreams*, fairly mediocre I admit, but enough to satisfy me: teeth that fall out = mourning; a full head of hair uncombed = worries; being pregnant = expectations; seeing a snake = betrayal; seeing a toad = victim of malicious gossip; wound on the body = an affront.

A pattern took shape. The travels I repeated in my dreams were not scholarly trips. I had not been invited by any cultural institution. I had not been in touch with any intellectuals or native readers. There was none of the frenzied or rowdy meetings as in Cuba or Israel. They were travels of a personal nature.

My first journey in my dreams took place in Indonesia. We had travelled to Indonesia for Richard's birthday. Depressed and delicate like all men, he thought that life stopped at fifty. I had reached that age well before him but couldn't convince him that he was still young. Despite spending hours at the Equinox gym on Broadway, he thought he was losing control of his body.

The journeys I repeated in my dreams were not very successful: perhaps because there were no personal contacts, and the sightseeing aspect took preference over the human element.

I had no control over these nocturnal imaginations. I found myself in the same position as Scheherazade in the *Arabian Nights*. My dream would abruptly come to an end in the morning with the first rays of sun. I would lie in bed, puzzled and frustrated.

In my dream, when we arrived, Indonesia was already marred by hordes of tourists. Real-estate developers were offering dream villas for next to nothing. Hoardings were advertising cheap discounts. We were amazed. For us, Bali was synonymous with magic. Yet everything was up for sale. It was not long before we discovered other aspects even more shocking. As we ventured off the beaten path, we came across a huge open-air rubbish tip from which household garbage, old objects and waste emitted a pestilential stench. We made a hasty departure in disgust. In our rush to leave, we passed groups of poorly dressed women with heavy receptacles on their heads like in Africa—they had been drawing water from a stream of murky, frothy, visibly polluted water. The island of the gods hid harrowing flaws.

Suddenly, everything changed. The day before we were to leave, I was gloomily soaking up the sun on one of the Sanur Beach Hotel beaches when winged messengers brought me an invitation to dinner with the sultan of Yogyakarta. I wasn't surprised since I

had been expecting something like that. The sultan
of Yogyakarta owned several palaces, including one
on Bali. In the evening, I dressed as best I could and
went out. I was alone but not concerned by Richard's
absence. I climbed into a luxury limousine waiting
for me at the entrance to the garden. For almost an
hour, we drove along a rough stony road. The moon
had risen and was playing hide and seek, peeping out
from time to time to show her finery. We arrived at
a landing stage where a group of sailors was waiting.
The sultan of Yogyakarta's palace rose up in the middle of a lake covered with immense lotus leaves from
which bloomed pink and white flowers. I reached an
island covered with a tangle of sweet-smelling roses,
jasmine and honeysuckle. The palace was a huge
white marble building, looking out onto the night
with brilliantly lit windows. Down below on the terrace meandered guests elegantly dressed in long
white silken tunics. The men had shaven heads in the
Muslim fashion; the women, however, had their hair
tied in heavy silky plaits. After a while, the sultan
himself appeared, also dressed in white, lying on a
canopied bed borne by his chamberlains. We settled
into deep and low, dark leather armchairs while
barefoot waiters glided about, placing dishes on
tables set beside us. After a number of appetizers
came the nasi goreng. I was not very fond of nasi
goreng composed of fried rice and slices of chicken.
I found it rather tasteless and reminded myself to
spice it up with shrimps once I was back in New
York. But when I tasted it, I found to my surprise

that it was very succulent, the best nasi goreng imaginable. I delved in and helped myself again and again. I stuffed myself under the sultan's indulgent eye.

'How do you like our cuisine?' he asked mischievously.

'It's the best in the world,' I replied, my mouth full.

'I've prepared a little surprise for you,' he smiled.

Whereupon he signalled to a waiter who brought me a parchment scroll, tied with a scarlet ribbon, on a silver tray. I opened it and discovered the recipe for nasi goreng. As I looked up to thank him, I realized the sultan had disappeared, together with his illustrious assembly. The orchestra's gamelan music had also faded. I was back in bed at Riverside Drive, eyes wide open in the dark.

The next journey in my dreams took me to Chile, in the absolutely opposite direction. We had travelled there three years previously. Since it was becoming increasingly difficult for me to walk and I needed a cane, Richard and I had the idea of going on a cruise from Fort Lauderdale in Florida to Valparaiso. It was the ship that would do the travelling and take me to the places I wanted to discover, such as Panama, Ecuador, Peru and Chile. Unfortunately, we hadn't foreseen the length of the decks nor the endless corridors between the cabins and the dining room, the smoking salon and the theatre. The lectures bored us. One in particular which attracted quite a crowd was devoted to the mixed fortunes of Princess Diana! We did not linger long on the chaise recliners on the promenade deck because of the icy breeze; we seldom went outside. It was only in the evenings that we watched with amusement the male escorts recruited and paid for by the cruise company raring to dance with the single women.

We never imagined that three weeks at sea could seem so long.

It was with a feeling of great relief that we reached Chile, our final port of call. Alas, I was immediately discouraged by the steps, lifts and hills of Valparaiso, no doubt a picturesque town but mostly inaccessible. Our lunch on a square, open to the four winds, was insipid and consisted of a cazuela, a kind of unappetizing vegetable bouillon. While we were having coffee, our Chilean friend, Hugo, a translator like Richard and whom we had met in Washington, came to fetch us. He apologized profusely for being on his own since his wife had to leave suddenly for Canada. He assured us, however, that he would make an excellent cicerone and show us the treasures of his native Santiago.

'Tomorrow,' he promised, dropping us off at our hotel, 'I'll take you to Pablo Neruda's house. You'll see, it's a sheer marvel.'

I'm ashamed to say I had never read much by Neruda. I had leafed through *Canto General*. A friend once gave me a collection of poems for my birthday called *Twenty Love Poems and a Song of Despair*. That's all.

His house had recently become a museum, known as La Chascona in honour of his last wife, a dazzling redhead. It had been built according to the plans designed by the poet himself. I should say it was less of a house and more a series of pavilions, built lopsided on steep slopes, connected by winding footpaths and tiny bridges. One of them housed Neruda's magnificent library. Another, bedrooms furnished in a baroque style and yet another, a string of sitting rooms. I especially admired one dining room whose walls were covered with tapestries and paintings and in the middle of which stood a monumental table of glazed tiles. La Chascona was perhaps a marvel, as Hugo said, but all I can remember is its complicated configuration.

Our stay in Santiago was not an agreeable one. My head was buzzing with the political dramas of 1973 and Pinochet's long dictatorship. But there was nothing to recall those years. At most, Santiago had the elegance of a Mediterranean city in the South of France. The crowds that jammed its streets, restaurants and bars seemed debonair and easygoing. Where had the spirit of Allende gone? Those years of resistance were nowhere to be seen. We had our meals in a small restaurant near the hotel. In order to keep to our budget, we always ordered the same dish, a kind of cottage pie.

The day before we left, a miraculous event happened: Mr and Mrs Lopez de Vega invited us for their wedding anniversary. The invitation was even more surprising since we had only met them once or twice at Hugo's; we barely knew them. Strangely enough, they weren't celebrating their anniversary at home but at La Chascona, in that dining room which had so impressed me. Mr Lopez de Vega turned out to be a great admirer of Allende and immersed in his memory.

When we arrived, the dining room was full of men and women talking and laughing loudly. A portrait of Allende hung on one of the walls framed by the national flag.

Mr and Mrs Lopez de Vega came over to us. 'Officially we're celebrating our wedding anniversary but in fact, it's for him. He is always in our memory.'

To say that the meal was excellent would be an understatement. *Empanadas al pino* and shrimps as big as langoustines were followed by brochettes of every kind of meat and fish accompanied by endless glasses of sparkling white wine and red wine tasting oddly of strawberries. There were also pyramids of fruit, especially lychees as big as a child's fist. A lychee tree once grew in our garden at Montebello. However hard we mistreated it, as the custom calls for, slashing its trunk, stabbing it with nails, it never bore any fruit. Suddenly, one July, it was covered in red fruit. We picked so many we had to give half to our neighbours.

'It's a bad omen,' predicted Ma Poirier, the owner of a storefront in Lower Montebello. Alas, it was true. A few months later, on 17 September, Guadeloupe was almost wiped off the face of the earth by the terrible hurricane Hugo.

Once again, the waiters refilled our glasses with pink champagne.

'We are going to raise a toast to him,' declared Mrs Lopez de Vega.

But the moment we raised our glasses, she vanished. I found myself in darkness. I could hear Richard breathing beside me. I had dreamt this voyage, and the dinner. I ended up going back to sleep, but, since the night was still young, I opened my eyes in Madagascar.

Since Françoise Vergès had invited me to talk about my books at the Regional Council of La Réunion, then presided over by her father, I couldn't help taking advantage of the opportunity to visit Madagascar, the nearby island where my daughter Sylvie worked as an economist. I had no inkling, though, that my stay would be catastrophic. Hardly had I stepped inside Sylvie's house than I took a nasty fall—I slipped in the middle of the dining room and dislocated my right knee. The physical therapist was sent for immediately who immobilized my leg in a cast. I therefore spent almost a week lying on a bed in a room where the air-conditioning was too high. Small consolation: Magdalen, Sylvie's cook, took pity on me and served up tasty little dishes. One day it was chicken cooked in coconut milk; another day, stuffed giant shrimps. One lunchtime, grinning like a hungry cat, she placed in front of me a small aluminium pot. 'It's a romazava,' she murmured mysteriously. 'Our national dish.'

I took a mouthful. It was a kind of beef stew cooked with a variety of brèdes, highly prized local herbs which gave the meat an unexpected, bitter taste. It was not to my liking and I was unable to finish it for cooking does not lend itself to politeness or pretence. Whatever the palate doesn't like, the throat cannot swallow nor the stomach digest. Visibly vexed, Magdalen removed her tray without a word.

When I was finally able to stand up, Jacques, Sylvie's chauffeur, took us on a drive to discover Antanarivo and its surroundings.

Madagascar is said to be a splendid island, and Sylvie never stopped singing its praises. The tourist brochures vaunted its landscapes, the colour of its sea and sky. For me, it was far from the truth. I was suffocated and blinded by it poverty. Emaciated men and women in rags sheltered in genuine pigsties. Some of them cultivated meagre plots of land with rudimentary tools. Sickly children stumbled along, carrying visibly malnourished babies on their backs. Everywhere I looked I saw utter destitution, far worse than I had seen in Guinea. Perhaps the years I had spent in the States had aggravated my sensitivity or squeamishness, call it what you like. Although there is no society more unequal than that of the States, one has to drive through the wretched neighbourhoods and ghettos in order to confront the destitute. Otherwise, poverty is not visible to the naked eye. In Madagascar, it's everywhere.

For a change of mood, Jacques ate up the 159 kilometres to Antsirabe, a thermal spa frequented in colonial times. The lucky few came to enjoy its mild climate. The sultan of Morocco, Mohammed V, spent part of his exile there. But instead of providing relief, Antsirabe made me even more depressed. Truly the world was divided into two unequal parts: the privileged, and the oppressed who never enjoyed a moment's pleasure. I became gloomier and gloomier.

Richard then had the idea of taking me to the natural park of Andasibe. Far from the urban areas which I loathed, I would be forced to focus on the dazzling beauty of nature. We booked a room at the Vakona Forest Lodge Hotel.

We arrived at nightfall and it was at that very moment that I was taken by the mysterious charm of the place. The trees shot up so high that they barred the sky, forming a canopy over the log bungalows scattered among the forest. We downed glasses of hot toddy in front of a blazing log fire. Alas, the following morning I had the bad idea of following Richard to admire the park's main attraction: the lemurs. They had been the subject of every conversation since New York. The lemurs apparently are endemic to Madagascar, and elude most predators. Together with a group of tourists, we first had to make our way for almost an hour through thick undergrowth. I stumbled along the spongy ground which sucked in the soles of my shoes at every step. We finally arrived at a small lake which we crossed in makeshift boats guided by the park rangers. The lemurs were parked out of harm's way on an island. Imagine the place, teeming with round-eyed animals as big as fair-sized tomcats, covered in silky black and white fur, and so familiar with humans that they jump onto your shoulders. I detest animals to such an extent that I have difficulty even being near cats and dogs. While the others took the opportunity to photograph each other hugging and stroking the lemurs, all I could think of was escaping. But frozen stiff from the cold morning, and horrified, I had to wait for the guides to decide when to return to the hotel.

After having survived that experience, we drove back double quick to Antanarivo. An Italian friend of Sylvie's invited us to a charity evening her foundation was hosting for underprivileged children. The ticket prices were exorbitant, but the stay in Madagascar had been such a flop that I unpacked my best dress and Richard his best suit. Although the foundation was secular, there was no hiding its religious orientation. The guest of honour was Father Pedro, an Argentinean priest from Slovenia who was to make a speech after dinner. Father Pedro was known internationally for having founded a number of orphanages in Madagascar. While waiting for him to begin his homily, waiters in traditional dress set down all kinds of appetizers and small aluminium pots in front of us. Even before opening them I guessed their contents: it was the famous ramazova, this time unrecognizable and deliciously savoury. Surprised, I helped myself several times. When the waiters cleared the tables, Father Pedro climbed up onto the stage. He was a handsome man with a thick beard and greying hair. His deep, resonant voice was unique.

'Let the little children come to me,' he exclaimed.

Then he described the incomparable and marvellous complicity between God and little children. I was soon transported as if I had heard God in person. I'm not a believer. Dragged to church, I yawned most of the time. But that evening, listening to that sublime voice, I felt stir in me a deep emotion. I realized that one shouldn't just be offended by the poverty in Madagascar but, rather, seek out its causes and denounce them. But how? My head was buzzing with ideas.

Suddenly I was again blinded by the darkness. I had imagined everything. I have to point out that this journey I had dreamt was not without consequences. The following morning I dashed to the university where I proposed writing an article for the campus newspaper. The editor looked me straight in the eye: 'You know you won't be paid,' she said.

I shrugged. 'I don't mind,' I replied. 'I simply want to make a contribution.'

My article was accepted and appeared the following month under the title 'Myth and Reality: My Trip to Madagascar'. Shortly afterwards I received a bittersweet letter from the association of Malagasy students at Columbia. It made a scathing attack on travellers who spend just a few days in a country and assume the right to become experts. I, nevertheless, had relieved my conscience.

For many months I dreamt a host of nocturnal imaginations but never a journey. Sometimes I was walking along the Hudson River, stopping at the pier for the Circle Line cruises. Sometimes I was climbing the steps of the Empire State Building to the platform where the tourists can admire the New York skyline. One day I ran the world-renowned New York marathon and joined the thousands of runners at the starting point on the Verrazano Bridge. I came in first, ousting the holder of the title, a certain Seneca Papagallo from Addis Ababa. The fact of the matter was that Seneca Papagallo was masquerading as an Ethiopian and was the son of a Guadeloupean couple, Rastafari disciples, who had answered the call of Haile Selassie. Seneca had grown up to the music of Tabou Combo and Kassav. He was so content with my victory he invited us both to celebrate at The Blue Moon, an Ethiopian restaurant in Brooklyn. I hadn't gone back to Brooklyn since the time of Adoremus. I felt the same nostalgia, since my stay in Macomb had not got me any closer to the African Americans. I remained far from that world of suffering and combat for which every minute of survival is a victory. Where was I when the police riddled the body of the unfortunate Amadou Diallo with forty-six bullets? What was I doing when another police squad shot and killed Sean Bell the night before his wedding outside the nightclub where he had come to throw his bachelor party? All these racist crimes of America, this America that was foreign to me but whose bursts of murderous voices I could hear from time to time, came home to suffocate me. Seneca's good mood however healed any of my usual misgivings. He was as familiar as Adoremus with the clubs in Brooklyn and took us to several of them.

Since my right leg was now useless, I was rid of the awful obligation to dance. I could remain seated at a table, drinking and laughing with my companions. When they disappeared onto the dance floor, I remained on my own, watching the men and women excel in an art I had never managed to master. As usual, I ended up recalling the events in my life and the all too short a time when my mother was alive, both hurting and delighting me with her presence.

When Seneca Papagallo left New York, he promised he would invite us to Ethiopia the following year. He did not keep his word. I received neither postcard nor letter or email from him, which was perfectly acceptable since he was merely a character out of my imagination. Yet I still have doubts. Hadn't I actually met that debonair giant with the dazzling smile?

Oddly enough, a dream brought the list of my voyages and imaginary revels to an end. I have always been enthusiastic about traditional Asian medicine. In Berkeley, I used to go to a massage centre in San Francisco. In New York, I was a regular visitor to the Salon de Tokyo where Japanese ladies trampled gaily on my legs and back. Then Dr Zhang Zhong burst into my life. He had been recommended to me by Marc Latamie, a painter from Martinique, who was treated by him for his allergies. A graduate from the faculty of medicine in Shanghai, his speciality was acupuncture and foot massage. Every week, he turned up at Riverside Drive. Bedecking my back with needles, he would talk to me about his childhood in the country, about his parents who were farmers and who had been ruined by a flood, their decision to leave for Shanghai and the difficulties they had making a place for themselves, then his exile to the States with the young girl he had just married and their painful adaptation in the borough of Queens.

Of course, he had made a success of his life. He owned a car and an apartment. He made a fortune from companies who were concerned about their staff's well-being. His daughter was completing her medical studies. Dr Zhang Zhong Li's English was not very good. His mouth emitted certain sounds which were totally incomprehensible. His hoarse, staccato, piercing voice, however, underwent a strange transformation. It became the voice of every immigrant, of every colour, who is forced into exile in order to survive but whose heart keeps intact his love for his native country. For Dr Zhang Zhing Li, China was a paradise. Every year he travelled to Shanghai where he had bought an apartment. Since US health care was too expensive, he and his family used the Chinese system for their annual check-up.

A few years earlier, his wife had been operated on for a cancer of the stomach. He had had all his teeth replaced, which gave him the dazzling white smile of a movie star. Since he still had an extended family in Shanghai, he insisted on organizing a stay for me.

One February, I was invited to a conference on Lafcadio Hearn in Tokyo and ended up accepting a stopover in Shanghai for a few days. My numerous invitations to universities in Tokyo, Kobe, Sapporo and Osaka had made me an ardent admirer of Japan. Its elegance and apparent serenity filled me with a feeling of respectful humility. As soon as I left the airport, I realized that China was something completely different. I had never witnessed such chaos. Men, women and teenagers were dashing to and fro, zigzagging on bicycles and scooters. Police officers, wearing ridiculous pith helmets, attempted in vain to control the traffic. Cars were heading in every direction and some had broken down in the middle of the road, creating traffic jams.

From the very start, Dr Zhang Zhong Li's organization proved to be far from perfect and this trip to China was doomed to failure. We were housed in an uncomfortable hotel, crowded with average Americans, the kind who are chatty and curious, prepared to engage in a conversation with perfect strangers about any subject, even the most private of topics. Meals were served in huge barrack-style halls where all the customers were foreigners. The food wasn't bad but you could have found better in any restaurants of the Monsoon chain in New York. In the end, we let Bob and Annette, a couple of restaurant owners from Pittsburg, get the better of us. For three years they had been coming to Shanghai, since Annette suffered from painful arthritis which the American physicians were unable to cure. They had an address book which I had no scruples using, with the names of acupuncturists, foot masseurs, hand masseurs as well as specialists in Japanese shiatsu, Thai boxing, t'ai chi and yoga. Great adepts of physical exercise, they dragged us on treks across town which lasted for hours. I limped along as best I could, always last.

'Don't be impressed by all this flashy modernity,' they told us, pointing out the hideous, ultramodern skyscrapers. 'There's another side to Shanghai. Some neighbourhoods are straight out of the Middle Ages.'

By way of proof they took us into neighbourhoods where little wooden houses painted brown huddled up against each other. Carefully kept little gardens alternated with beds of tulips, dahlias and vegetable plots. It was the China straight out of the Vermot almanac. You were almost expecting to pass men with long plaits dangling down their backs. The sight of me every time caused a riot. People crowded out on their doorsteps to stare. But it was not the humiliating sneers I had suffered in India. Nor was it the indifference of the Indonesians. These were warm smiles and friendly gestures. Everyone wanted to shake my hand or have a picture taken with me. The few who spoke English asked for my address.

Bob and Annette took us to the Bund, the former financial heart of the city lined with the major banks and foreign trading houses. It was a surprising place located along the river Huangpu. In the evening, the illuminated boats that drifted along turned it into an enchanted wonderland. The Bund overflowed with restaurants which were out of bounds to us since they did not accept our meal tickets. I watched with envy the elegant diners stepping out of their limousines, the men dressed in Mao suits, buttoned up to the collar, the women draped in designer dresses. I was particularly impressed by the constant ballet of limousines in front of the Blue Elephant restaurant whose large terrace swept down to the river where waiters were busy serving the guests. I was determined to have a full meal there before leaving Shanghai. But our farewell evening turned out to be very different from what I had imagined.

As I was gingerly climbing down the steps of the hotel with Richard, we were approached by a young man, twenty or twenty-five years old, dressed in a traditional tunic and wide linen trousers.

'My name is Lin Pao. My mother has sent me to invite you to dinner,' he smiled. He spoke perfect English. 'Will you do her the honour? She will be so pleased.'

We looked at each other in surprise. His mother? Who was she?

'She knows all about you,' the young stranger continued looking at me. 'She has read all your books.'

Then he turned to Richard and added: 'At least those that your husband has translated into English.'

No emissary could have been more gracious. Devoured by curiosity, we followed him to a bus stop where I made the usual impression. But I had eyes only for Shanghai by night, blazing with the lights from its billboards and signs.

After half an hour we reached one of those neighbourhoods untouched by modernity where little houses lined alleyways as if straight out of a child's drawing. One of them was brilliantly lit, its doors and windows wide open. A crowd was waiting for us and exchanged greetings, even kisses, as if our long-lost friends.

The young man's mother introduced herself. 'My name is Piu Dong.' Then she clasped me to her breast and whispered. 'I too am a writer. I write children's books. But since my husband is a well-known opponent, the books have been banned by the regime. My sole wish is to collect enough money to join my husband who has fled to South Korea to escape prison. Before we start to eat the dishes we have prepared for you, let us drink a toast to freedom of expression which does not exist here.'

We drank to the freedom of expression and then took our seats around the table. Chinese cuisine has made a name for itself worldwide. Even those who have never tasted it have heard about shark-fin soup, Peking duck or chicken with black mushrooms. What makes the difference is the succulence of these commonplace dishes. I shall never forget the meal we had in that humble dwelling surrounded by strangers with smiling faces. First came a soup of asparagus tips and shrimp; then seafood fritters followed by a sort of Chinese paella the likes of which I had never tasted. Piu Dong was seated to my right. Occasionally we shook hands affectionately. I shall never know why but this was the last meal of my dreams.

When did Paris become a rainy city? I couldn't say. When I leaf through the album of my memories, be they happy or unhappy, they are always filled with sunlight. I always used to think of Paris as truly the City of Light. During the day, the sun was the source of a blaze of light; in the evening, the streetlights and lamps along the pavements glowed continually. When I was young, I loved to walk. I would walk at a brisk pace from my students' residence on the rue Lhomon to the lycée Fénelon on the rue de l'Epéron, near the Saint-André-des-Arts crossroads. At noon, I would walk back up to the Institute of Hispanic Studies, on the rue Gay-Lussac where my friend Jocelyne was studying for her BA in Spanish. My friendship with Jocelyne bordered on passion. Dark-skinned, with a dark mop of hair since she had Indian blood, she had grown up in the various colonies where her father practised as magistrate, notably in Senegal. She possessed a fascinating aura of cosmopolitanism and an assurance which made me ashamed of my own lack of confidence.

Since we both had a common contempt for the university restaurants where the food was insipid and served up in ugly metal trays, we would amble up to the Gobelins neighbourhood. Wedged up against the famous bar, Le Canon, was a small Turkish cafe where they sold kebabs which we thought rare and original before they became commonplace in Paris. Since the restaurant was no bigger than a pocket handkerchief, we would sit outside in the sun and eat our sandwiches on a bench. Jocelyne would declaim in her lovely warm voice lines from her favourite poet, Nicolas Guillen:

> *Aqui hay blancos y negros y chinos y*
> *mulatatos*
> *Desde luego, se trata de coloures baratos,*
> *Pues a través, de tratos y contraltos*
> *Se han corrido los tintes y no hay un tono*
> *estable.*

Men passing by would whistle lasciviously at us seated side by side or make indecent gestures. Secretly, I was delighted even though I pretended to be outraged like Jocelyne. Here I was, suddenly an object of lust and desire. Little did I realize that this transformation was simply due to exoticism.

Likewise, when I visited my sisters, I would walk to the Gare du Nord to catch a bus to their place. At that time, the buses were open at the back. Influenced by Aragon whose novel *Les Voyageurs de l'impériale* (The Passengers on the Double-Decker Bus) I had read over and over, I never sat inside but preferred to stand outside. I would watch intently everything that was going on around me. I was born

on a small sleepy island. There were few cars on the
road except for the charabancs whose drivers chal-
lenged each other to races and often ended up in the
ditch. Here I was catapulted into a colourful, noisy
and bustling metropolis. I had no reason to be scared
of Paris since I hadn't yet lived those later painful
events. I was pleasantly excited. Whenever I had time
on my hands, I would wander as far as the Gare du
Nord. I loved this railway station. The sunlight
bounded through the glass roof, flooding with light
the crowds of travellers rushing to and fro like ants,
zigzagging here and there, loaded with children,
boxes and luggage. Who were they? Where did they
come from? Where were they going? This mysterious
and unfathomable agitation never ceased to attract
me, like life itself.

It was under a blazing sun that, together with my
sisters, I accompanied Sandrino cramped into a varnished wooden coffin to the airport at Orly. Air
France had recently replaced the train from Le
Havre. I was unable to sob like my sisters. I could
imagine my mother's grief. She died a few months
later, probably from a broken heart and oblivious to
the fact that she had other children to care for. I often
wonder what my life would have been like if my
mother hadn't died so early. As things stand, I feel an
immense void, an enormous gaping wound. She has
never sat any of my children on her knees. She has
never heard word of my first marriage to Condé. She
has no idea I have become a writer. Would she have
liked my books? Would she have appreciated the

way I described her? Would I have written *Victoire, My Mother's Mother* if she had still been alive? Her absence has been such a huge influence on me. What would her presence have done?

It was also under the sun that I have been twice married. Both times under the sun? I am sure the sun was shining during the first wedding, despite its painful ending. Snapshots testify to it, and show a small group, smiling appropriately, standing with their backs to the leafy plane trees on the square in front of the Eighteenth District town hall in Paris. The second time, I'm not so sure. I prefer to focus on the white cotton ensemble ordered for next to nothing from an online catalogue of the Trois Suisses. Was I really so hard-up? In any case, it makes a good impression in the wedding album Richard and I are so proud of.

It was also under the sun that I had my son cremated at Père Lachaise, surrounded by a group of mourners whose hearts could not contain the extent of their grief. Jacques Martial read a beautiful poem while we were all lost in prayer in the funeral parlour. A few months later, my daughter Aïcha took the urn containing Denis' ashes to Guadeloupe. Since my brother was now ill and bedridden, I had to conduct the delicate negotiations with my sister-in-law in order to obtain a place in the spacious family vault in Basse-Terre. I realize now that I revived their grief. One year before, they had buried their thirty-year-old son, George, who had lost control of his car and crashed into a mango tree along the straight and narrow road leading to Morne-à-L'Eau. In the end, it was on George's coffin that we set the urn containing his cousin's remains, both snatched too early from their loved ones. The memory of that macabre ceremony haunts me even today.

To conclude on a happier note, it was one sunny afternoon that I learnt of the birth of Raky, my first granddaughter. It was election day in France. The Socialists were ecstatic. The changeover of power had been achieved and Mitterand elected president. Yves Benot's statement that 'Right or Left, a mother country remains a mother country' discouraged me from being overjoyed at these political ups and downs. I had but one thought in mind: of this fragile little girl emerging into this terrible life from which, as the African proverb says, you don't get out alive.

Once Paris had changed into a grey, drizzly city where the wind and the rain gave way to sudden showers, my first thoughts were to escape. Although winter in New York is often bitterly cold, at least the sun shines high in the sky. Weak and lukewarm, it radiates just a little brightness. Until recently, I knew very little about France, except for the Mont Saint-Michel which my parents adored for some unknown reason. I think they spent their honeymoon there or something similar. Consequently, as a child and later as an exasperated and sulky teenager, I had to sit in a rental car which my father drove at forty kilometres per hour, stalling and fumbling with the gears while repeating loudly every other minute: 'There's no denying it! France is a beautiful country!'

His voice betrayed the admiration and alienation of the colonized. When my parents dragged me to the Mont Saint-Michel, I was not impressed by this strange rocky island, sometimes its feet immersed in water, other times perfectly dry. Among the throngs of visitors were a large number of nuns in winged cornets and priests in cassocks. The Italian priests wore elegant felt hats which I loved. My mother dragged me into the basilica where a priest offered his ring to be kissed. A choir of seminarians was singing the 'Stabat Mater' by Pergolesi. Despite my bad mood, I was transported.

When Paris changed in nature, Richard and I changed our routine. We would hire a car and venture into the unknown. We were not afraid of distances and ate up motorways and highways. I particularly liked visiting Madeleine Hage who had restored a former silkworm factory at La Bruyère in the Cevennes not far from the little town of Ganges whose Sunday market sold a wide variety of spices, including saffron, curcuma, coriander, cumin and the ras-el-hanout spice blend. Madeleine and I organized culinary tournaments. Her speciality was coq au vin, the traditional French dish, much to the delight of Jerry, her husband, and his American palate. I preferred jambalaya or tajines. Sometimes, an English neighbour brought in a fish curry and we would sit down in the yard in a festive mood and eat under a slowly darkening patch of sky.

I also liked going to Nice, to our friend Amy who divided her time between Washington and France. Since she was a fervent enthusiast of Picard's frozen foods, unfortunately there was no culinary contest between us.

We also drove in the opposite direction and headed north to Letizia Galli's place at the Roches Noires in Trouville, in a block of flats where the memory of Marguerite Duras still lingers. Although Richard loved this beach, which reminded him of the one he used to run along as a child, I had my reservations since Trouville is far from sunny. I must confess, however, that the few times when the sun poked its head out of the clouds, everything was transformed and endowed with a surprising beauty. The sea assumed those sumptuous hues which have enthralled so many painters. There were no culinary contests with Letizia either. She could only tolerate Italian cuisine, notably mussels and asparagus tips risotto or a salad of white beans mixed with shrimps.

One day, I was intrigued by a letter in the mail. Nothing unusual, except it bore the odd heading: Ouessant, last point of call in Brittany before America. These words were like a mysterious summons. I slit it open out of curiosity and it contained an invitation to a festival on the island of Ouessant. I had only been to Brittany once or twice: to Douarnenez and the house of Simone Gallimard who was not only my editor but also a sincere and generous friend; and to Saint-Malo where I had been invited to the literary festival Etonnants Voyageurs.

I might have refused this invitation but for the coincidence of watching a TV documentary on the islands of Brittany: Bréhat, Batz, Belle-Ile-en Mer, Ouessant, Molène and Groix. Richard was overjoyed at seeing so much natural beauty and our minds were made up, despite the disgruntled comments of some.

'You hate the grey and the rain, yet you're going to Brittany. Don't say we didn't tell you!'

We went even so.

This time we thought it sensible to take the train. We weren't expecting anything great from Brest which we knew had been bombed to ruins in the Second World War and then rebuilt without any originality. But as soon as we arrived at the little port of Conquet a miracle happened. While the sun dazzled overhead and the boat danced and rolled over the sea, all my fantasies flowed back in a rush. Perhaps I haven't talked enough about the sea and the mixed feelings it inspires in me. It's true, it frightens me because of all the nonsense Adélia and Michelle filled my head with when we were children. But above all its boundless immensity impresses me. It takes nothing but a breath of wind to make it furious. At night, its laugh, like that of a mad woman goes the Antillean proverb, sweeps under the bed covers.

When I used to go with my parents to the beach at Viard, I refused to look at the waves. Huddled up in a ball, I dreamt of burying my head in the sand.

'I don't know what the child is scared of!' my mother lamented, coating her arms with palma-christi oil which was an ersatz for sunscreen. 'How will she ever be able to deal with life?'

Yes, how have I been able to deal with life? After watching *The Big Blue*, I was haunted by a recurring nightmare: lost in the ocean's depths, I was struggling as best I could between a coral reef and a school of jellyfish. I brushed against fish while white sharks showed me their teeth. Not out of aggressiveness but in a kind of cruel grin. Utter darkness. Not a sound. I was certainly going to die at the bottom of this liquid tomb. Yet, at the same time, the ocean fascinates me. I love it. Scientists tell us that one day it will cover the planet and its empire will be boundless. The earth will be cleansed of its pettiness, its meanness, its suffering and mourning. Nobody knows where Guadeloupe and Martinique will end up. Great slabs covered with barbaric-looking flowers will drift over the water. Humans will no longer exist. It's because of all this confusion that I called one of my later novels *En attendant la montée des eaux* (Waiting for the Waters to Rise). The story takes place in Haïti whose misfortunes we are all familiar with. The characters too are sorely afflicted. What I meant was that everything is temporary, that another time will come, bringing peace and happiness.

On the ferry that took us to Ouessant, a writer whose face was familiar but whose name I couldn't remember, came and sat beside us. 'This crossing is one of the most dangerous that exists,' he told us. 'There's no counting the number of shipwrecks. Worst are the sudden, violent squalls that take the helpless sailors by surprise.'

Despite these hardly optimistic words, we arrived safe and sound at Ouessant. A group was waiting for us on the jetty, including an old man dressed like a druid who turned out to be the father of the festival's director. Under the guidance of this strange personage, we made our way to the centre of the island. The festival was held under a huge tent which also served as a refectory. The meetings took place in the welcoming centre, a stone building, probably a village hall, next door. Young servers dressed in pretty traditional costumes handed out bowls of cider, meat pâtés and stuffed shrimps. Among the festival-goers I was overjoyed to meet again my old friend, the Haitian Rodney Saint-Eloi. Settled in Canada, he is the director of a publishing house, Mémoire d'Encrier, which published a book of mine for young adults, *Conte Cruel*.

I was also bombarded by a Martinican woman who promised to cure me: 'Let me help you!' she cried. 'I'll help you get rid of that cane. Once the festival's over, you'll be trotting around like a billy goat.'

From that moment on, she came and dragged me out of bed every morning. Unfortunately, her massages and laying on of hands had no effect whatsoever.

I fell in love with Ouessant not only because of the island's wild and spectacular beauty but also because of the festival's ambiance. It was a simple, good-natured meeting. None of the participants took themselves seriously nor treated the others with superior airs. Up on stage, the main focus was literature but it was discussed with humility since everyone knows that the god of Literature is Tolerance and gladly accepts all those who bow before her. The festival's theme was: Does a Literature of the Islands Exist? I personally don't think so. It would mean giving too much importance to a geographical origin and not sufficiently taking into account the many facets that form a writer's personality. To be born in Guadeloupe, on a land surrounded on all sides by water, as the old school manuals used to say, is less important for me than having lived for many years in America where I found my 'freedom of expression'.

On the very first evening, we stepped into the pub the Ty Korn where Ronan, the owner, served an excellent rum punch. I have said that I'm not keen on rum. But sipping a rum punch on a windy night to the plaintive sounds of the fog horn in such a particular context . . . I felt the same way as I had coming across an old acquaintance in Tokyo years earlier.

Ronan came and sat next to me. 'For two years I knocked about the islands on a banana boat,' he told me. 'My favourite is Saint Barts. Have you been there? When you lot complain about colonization, we Bretons are the first to understand, even those of us who never left Brittany. The authorities were determined to strip us of our language, to hound it out of our schools. The children who dared speak it were severely punished. Every aspect of our culture has been ridiculed and despised. You must have heard the jokes about the Breton Bécassine, the silly goose. They've made us out to be alcoholics. They've mocked our belief in the supernatural, in everything that is not materialistic and for profit.'

I listened to him in surprise. And by way of homage to this budding friendship, I downed a second rum punch which sent me straight home.

Every evening there was an event for our enjoyment. Once, there was a concert of Celtic music which excited my attention. Another time, quite unexpectedly, a young group from Guadeloupe and Martinique living in Quimper played until the early hours of the morning. Maëva, the singer, claimed she had read all my books, a little white lie which pleased me. I had never had the opportunity to talk to a second generation of Antilleans, so I had no scruples taking advantage of the situation.

'I've always asked myself what it would be like to be born in France and consider this country one's own.'

'What difference does it make if you're born there or in France? Guadeloupe is a French department.'

I attempted to explain what my generation had felt regarding one's identity. She frowned, unconvinced. 'Does that mean you feel African? Or American?'

We were invited to dinner at some neighbours', a couple of elementary-school teachers, Mahel and Anne, who lived in Lorient during the school year. Knee high to a grasshopper and her face wrinkled like a potato Anne talked to me like a true schoolmistress. 'Breton cuisine,' she declared, 'goes straight to the essentials. It makes a point of preserving the original qualities of each product: skate, crabs and whelks.'

Then she softened her tone of voice. 'What made you become interested in cooking?'

'I don't know. It's like asking me how I became interested in writing. I started to cook at the same time I learnt to write and count.'

After that we went over to the dining room table where numerous dishes had been set out.

'I've made you some mackerel rillettes,' she said, lifting one lid. 'Because the mackerel is not expensive, it tends to be looked down on. But it's a wonderful fish with its white, savoury flesh. Much better than salmon over which there is so much fuss.'

Her rillettes were excellent.

'Let's go on to the Ouessant custard flan. It's a typical recipe of the island. In the past, people used to cook their flan in the fireplace.'

She cut a slice with a worried look. 'A good flan,' she said, 'must be moist inside and crusty around the edge and on top.'

After tasting it, she seemed satisfied and piled our plates with a slice. In the meantime, Mahel had been constantly filling our glasses with cider.

'We always spend Christmas on Ouessant with our two daughters and their family,' he told us. 'You should come here in winter, not in the summer when the tourists on their bikes clutter up our roads and beaches. In winter, there are scarcely more than five hundred inhabitants. The entire island and the ocean become one.'

Without doubt, the most spectacular night drive was the visit to the lighthouses, especially to the Creach lighthouse, one of the most powerful in the world. When we left the village, not a star was in the sky. Only the headlights of our minivan pierced the darkness. Nobody said a word. Our lips were squeezed tight in fright. I thought I could see the shapes of prehistoric animals scamper around us. I was rooted to my seat. The lighthouses suddenly reared up along the coast like monuments wrapped in thick mist. Their glaring eyes swept over the sea and the horizon. Standing in front of the Creach lighthouse, we found ourselves reduced to insignificance before its rotating dazzle. Facing the unknown, we felt the mysterious call of space in all its immensity. I remembered the expression which had so intrigued me: Ouessant, last call in Brittany before America. It was true. We were really standing on the edge of the earth.

I became passionate about Ouessant, however, when Ronan told me its history one evening as we sat quietly drinking rum punch in the Ty Korn.

'In the nineteenth century,' he told me, 'Ouessant was nicknamed the Island of Women. The island at that time was inhabited solely by brave, hard-working women, dressed in black, who sat in church on Sundays with their babies in their arms. You see, the ocean is too violent in these parts for a fisherman to earn a living. So the men had to engage in the merchant navy and sail off to the other side of the world. They remained there for months before they returned to the island. During the Second World War, when the Germans occupied Ouessant for its strategic location, they had no trouble seducing all these lonely women who were attracted by their uniforms and black-market goods. I can't tell you how many German descendants there are hiding among us. At the end of the war, none of the women had their heads shaved in public. Everything was kept a secret.

'Are there any books on the subject?' I asked. 'I'd be interested to read them.'

He shrugged. 'Certainly not,' he shouted. 'No one has written on the subject. As a novelist, you know full well that you can't always tell the truth.'

I sighed. 'No, unfortunately! Readers prefer uplifting stories that are largely lies: myths in other words.'

By virtue of these secrets, Ouessant changed its personality. It was no longer simply that beautiful island set in the sea with its strikingly wild nature, but the scene of many a drama that had been played out behind closed doors.

The day before we left, there was a crazy evening of entertainment at the Ty Korn where everyone improvised some music, a poem or a song. Despite my fear of looking ridiculous, I composed a kind of prose poem, incredibly lyrical, in which I expressed the sensations I had felt during my stay. The audience of Bretons was delighted. One woman came up to shake my hand, her eyes filled with tears. 'It's wonderful what you have just said,' she whispered.

Around ten in the evening, Ronan's wife, who worked in Quimper during the week and only returned to Ouessant on weekends, invited a group of privileged customers into her kitchen. She had made a stew in an iron pot wrapped in peat.

'It's the peat,' she explained to me, 'that gives this dish its particular taste and consistence. It can't be made anywhere else.'

Thereupon she gave me a little book where the recipes seemed to be handwritten. It was called *Breton Cook*. She was right. Back home, I was unable to make any of the recipes which were either too complicated or too elaborate, requiring components I don't have. I have kept it safely shelved among my books and no longer open it.

The following morning, we took the ferry which brought us back to the continent after a stopover in Molène. Le Conquet and then Brest were drowning in rain whereas Paris was gasping for breath from a heatwave that had taken everyone by surprise.

Ouessant remains one of my most pleasant memories. The island taught me a lesson: there's no need to travel long distances, huddled in a plane for hours in order to discover something new. This small patch of land, a stone's throw from the coast of France, possesses a singular and endearing personality. Where does the character we endow a place or ourselves with come from, I asked myself? I don't have a set answer to that. But I do remember a visit to Bermuda at the start of my university career. Bermuda has the particularity of being a British possession off the shores of America as if the founding fathers hadn't dared approach it. But if I was expecting a staggering mix of British and American traditions, I was to be disappointed. Except for the long shorts cut off at the knee and the thick woollen socks the men wear, the island seemed to have invented nothing. At the conference's opening gala, a singer sang through a list of Frank Sinatra's old songs. The movie evening was devoted to Clint Eastwood, a filmmaker I especially loathe. The meals consisted of the worst type of hamburgers: gravelly minced meat, tasteless tomato slices and spongy, badly defrosted buns. After much reflection I came to the conclusion that it needs oppression and consequently rebellion in order to create an authentic culture. The inhabitants of Bermuda are too rich, too affluent and too content with their island.

By Way of Summing Up

I have always refused to rank my two passions but nowadays I am forced to admit that one of them has an outstanding superiority over the other. As a writer gets older, she lives in fear of rambling and repeating over and over the same book. Since she is haunted by the same obsessions and obsessed by the same thoughts and concerns, one question inevitably recurs. 'Haven't I already told this story? In which book was it?'

In order to reassure herself, all she need do is reread her books but she recoils at such an unpleasant task.

For the cook, on the contrary, repetition is proof of excellence. When my friends demand: 'Make that dish you do so well,' I am overjoyed and get down to business. When I am in Paris, I hobble as far as the Passage Brady, a paradise of exotic flavours. When I'm in New York, the Whole Foods supermarkets make life easier. Jambalaya gets the loudest applause, a dish originating from Louisiana, a mixture of chicken, salt pork, sausage, shelled shrimps and red or black beans. I've lost count of the number of times I have shared the recipe. Leila, my difficult third daughter, never wants anything else for her birthday.

I recently suffered a false hope. Mounir, the only male amid a large brood of grandchildren, told me he would like to be a chef and asked for a number of recipes. A chef! I was delighted and immediately imagined him wearing a white chef's hat, busily giving orders to a crowd of assistants. What would his father think, a traditional Senegalese officer working for an international organization? What would my daughter, his mother, think,0   who had tried her hand at Sciences-Po? Would she accept such a vocation for her only son?

I set to work, since it is not easy for me to write down recipes which I only know how to improvise and taste over and over again in order to achieve a dish's perfection. I did as best I could and went to a great deal of trouble. Alas, when I had finished and telephoned Mounir, he told me with the fickleness of his age that he had changed his mind and was planning on doing something else. Nevertheless, he kindly offered to cook me a meal since he boasted he was an excellent cook. Consequently, even in this field, I shall be at a loss for an heir.